COUNTRY
CROSS STITCH

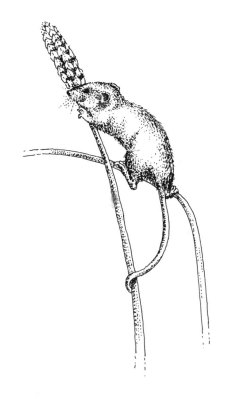

COUNTRY CROSS STITCH

55 Charts with More Than 100 Designs

JANE GREENOFF

Have communion with few,
Be familiar with one,
Deal justly with all,
Speak evil of none.

from a sampler by
Sarah Hubbard 1845

THE READER'S DIGEST ASSOCIATION, INC.
Pleasantville, New York/Montreal

To Bill, always

THE INGLESTONE COLLECTION

The Inglestone Collection produces counted cross-stitch kits including some of the designs in this and previous books by Jane Greenoff.

The books and kits are available from Designing Women Unlimited, 601 East Eighth Street, El Dorado, Arkansas 71730 USA; tel: (501) 862-0021.

Jane Greenoff founded the Guild in 1996 to promote the enjoyment of counted needlework of all kinds to embroiderers around the world. For details of subscriptions, members' facilities and further information contact: The Cross Stitch Guild, The Stable Courtyard, Longleat House, Warminster, BA12 7NW, England.

A Reader's Digest Book

Edited and Produced by David & Charles Publishers

Library of Congress Cataloging in Publication Data

    Greenoff, Jane.
       Country cross stitch: 55 cross stitch charts with more than 100
    designs/Jane Greenoff.
         p.   cm.
       "First published in Great Britain in 1992"—T.p. verso.
       includes index.
       ISBN 0-89577-967-6
       1. Cross-stitch—Patterns.   2. Decoration and ornament, Rustic.
    I. Title.
    TT778.C76G75165   1997
    746.44'3041—dc21   97–3328

Printed and bound in Great Britain.

Contents

Introduction

The idea for this country chart book came quite unintentionally! After finishing my second cross stitch book, I took time to enjoy our Cotswold cottage and the lovely countryside around us. However, living in the country and being a self-confessed cross stitch addict, I suppose the consequences were probably inevitable, as the countryside and the images it creates lends itself to all forms of embroidery, but particularly to counted cross stitch – the greatest problem when the ideas came thick and fast was where to stop!

This book is intended for cross stitch enthusiasts everywhere, with pages of colored charts, all with a country theme, that can be used for cross stitch on both even-weave fabrics and canvas. Many of the charts can be adapted for work on canvas using yarn and/or stranded floss; where appropriate, an exchange chart for Paterna yarn has been included. Which canvas type is used has been left to personal choice and the needs of the end product. All that needs to be checked is the number of strands needed to cover the canvas effectively; you will find it helpful to work a small test area if you are not familiar with the yarn.

How to complete some of the more complicated projects is described in Useful Techniques (page 115).

THE CHARTS

All the charts in the book have been used in some form in the projects photographed, either in individual items or as part of a larger project.

Each motif on the charts is numbered, as are the charts themselves. You will see from the photographs throughout the book that some of the designs have been used more than once, thus demonstrating the adaptability of charted needlework. This simple system of numbering the motifs and charts will help you find your way around the charts, and it makes it easy to select the motifs you need for the larger projects. For example, to stitch the tree sampler on page 41 you will need border 13 on chart 2 (page 13), garland motifs 74 and 75 on chart 34 (page 78), the alphabet on chart 17 (page 42), the tree motif on chart 18 (page 43), and the apple motif 103 (page 112).

The charts are all in color, and the color key on the chart itself is noted in DMC shade numbers unless stated otherwise. This number refers to the shade used for the stitched model in the color picture. You will find threads in alternative colors also listed in the text; these have been specially selected to suit each project and to blend with each other, so you may see more than one alternative shade for any color. In a few cases, no suitable alternatives are shown because this is just not possible.

THE FABRICS

A number of different fabrics have been used in the worked examples in the photographs, all of which should be readily available in good needlework stores or possibly by mail order. Where the type of fabric is of particular importance to the completed project, it will be mentioned at the beginning of the section, although a complete list of fabrics used can be found on page 114. As already mentioned, you should feel free to experiment with your own ideas and any spare pieces of material you have carefully saved! When you select a piece of fabric for a particular design, check the thread count of your material and the stitch count of the design you have chosen. This is most important if the completed project has to fit a particular frame, card, or jar lid.

THREADS

If you want to duplicate the effect shown in the color photographs, you must use the colors and threads shown on the color charts, which are also denoted by * in the text. The other lists of threads are provided for those who prefer to use other brands of thread.

DMC stranded floss is a six-ply mercerized thread which is usually divided into the number of strands most appropriate for the design and the fabric of your choice.

German flower thread (GFT) is a single-ply, unmercerized cotton thread which is used singly for cross stitch and gives the work an attractive matte finish. It can be very effective to contrast the two types of yarn in one project. In some designs you may prefer to outline the cross stitch in one strand of stranded floss instead of flower thread to produce a more delicate finish.

Paterna yarn, a pure virgin wool spun and dyed in England, has a beautiful rich luster. This three-ply yarn is very adaptable and can be combined with stranded floss to good effect.

Designer silk is space-dyed by hand and blended throughout the spectrum, so that the color changes are delicate and subtle. Each length gradually changes color, from a dark shade at one end to a lighter shade at the other, so the stitcher can work subtle color changes without continuously changing threads. The yarn is sold in mixed skeins, often including more than one color or shade. When working cross stitch with Designer Silk, it is important that each cross stitch be worked individually rather than in two directions.

WASHING AND PRESSING
CROSS STITCH

When a project is complete, check for skipped stitches and loose ends. If necessary, the design may be washed by hand in hot water with a soap-based product, rinsed well, and dried naturally. To press cross stitch, cover the ironing board with a thick, soft white towel and press the needlework on the wrong side with a hot iron. NEVER press cross stitch on the right side as you will flatten all your efforts!

NB Standard measurements are used throughout, with metric equivalents in parentheses.

Things to do

Sun   a.m.   p.m.

Mon

Tue

Wed

Thur

Fri

Borders

Many cross stitch designs use a stitched border to "frame" the picture, although it depends both on personal choice and the type of project you are planning. These two pages of charts can be used on your own designs or combined with other charts in the book to make some of the illustrated models.

 The color codes for these charts refer to the thread used for the border designs throughout the book.

CHART 1

Pink Carnation (motif 1)

Color	*GFT	DMC	ANCHOR	PATERNA
Cherry	2088	3350	0896	903
Rose pink	2068	335	038	905
Sage green	3001	320	0261	602
Medium green	2000	989	0241	613

Corner A (motif 2)

Color	GFT	*DMC	ANCHOR	PATERNA
Green	3902	937	0263	601

Corner B (motif 3)

Color	GFT	*DMC	ANCHOR	PATERNA
Pale green	2099	772	0259	614
Medium green	2001	988	0262	612
Dark green	3902	937	0263	601

Red and Blue Borders (motifs 4, 5, and 6)

Color	GFT	*DMC	ANCHOR	PATERNA
Pink	2041	3350	0896	903
Blue	3122	930	0851	511
Green	2001	988	0262	612

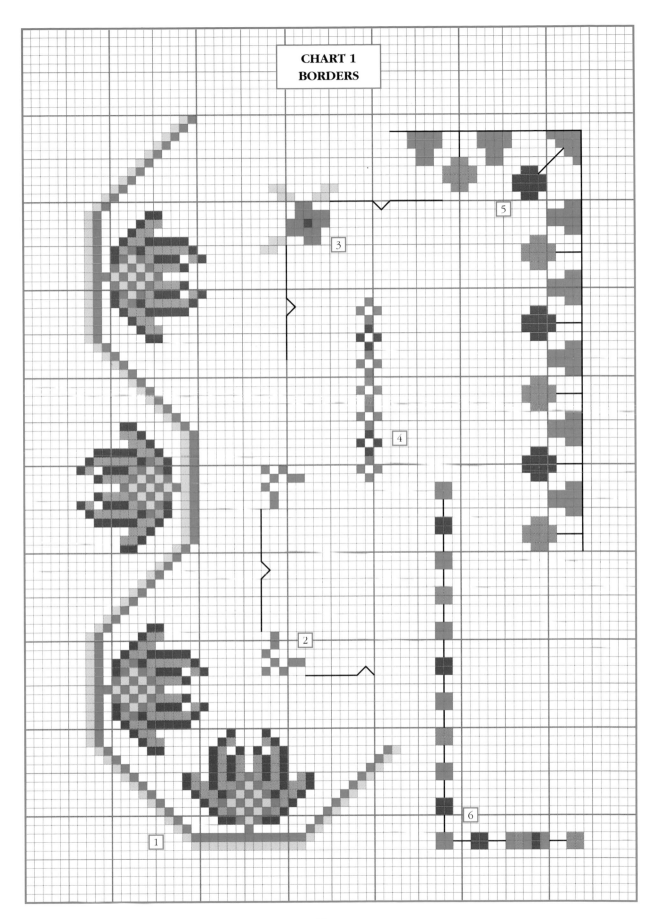

CHART 2

Single-color borders (motifs 7 and 8)

These simple borders can be stitched in any color, in any yarn, and are often useful around a simple design as shown on page 41, the little alphabet.

Flower borders (motifs 9 and 12)

These two pretty little designs are not seen stitched in the book, but could be used as an alternative to suggested borders.

Traditional strawberries (motif 10)

Color	GFT	*DMC	ANCHOR	PATERNA
Dark green	3902	937	0263	600
Light green	3001	989	0261	602
Honey	2003	738	0372	405
Purple	2011	327	0872	321

Pink and Blue Stars (motif 11)

Color	GFT	*DMC	ANCHOR	PATERNA
Cornflower	3403	340	0118	342
Pale blue	1022	341	0117	343
Pink	1002	335	038	904

Blue carnation (motif 13)

Color	GFT	*DMC	ANCHOR	PATERNA
Dark blue	3722	930	0851	511
Light blue	1022	932	0850	513
Dark green	3902	501	0878	532
Light green	2099	503	0875	523

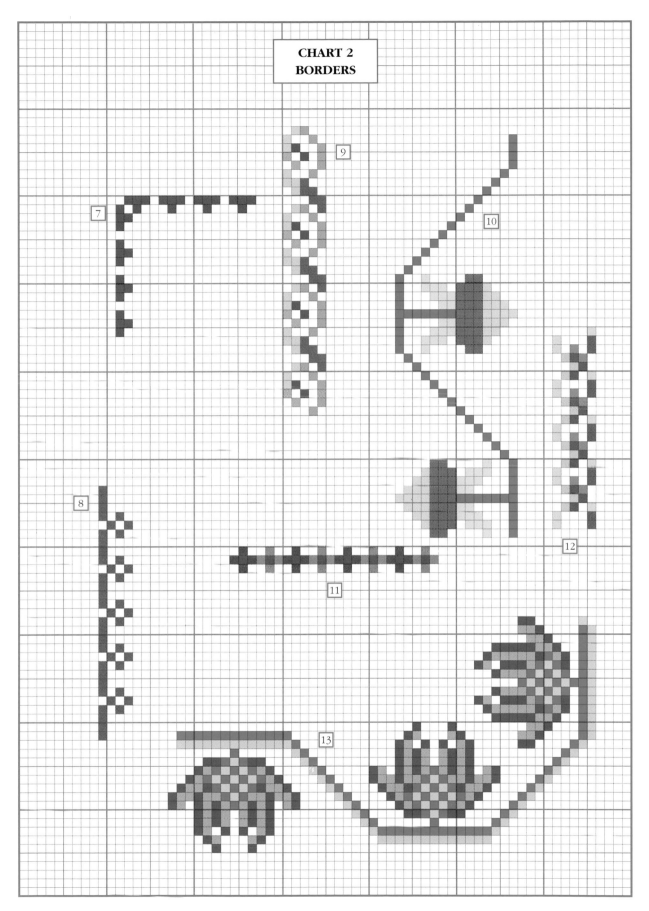

Butterflies, Birds, Harvest, and Hedges

Although wildlife is a little more difficult to work in cross stitch, the finished effect can be quite charming. The designs on the following pages have been made as the butterfly and ladybug alphabet, James's country diary, the silk thread file, and the butterfly crystal jar illustrated on page 16.

CHART 3

BUTTERFLIES

The butterfly is always a popular motif for both counted cross stitch and needlepoint. These pretty designs can be used alone or combined with other designs illustrated on page 16. A butterfly stitched in stranded floss for the lid on a crystal jar has been made according to the manufacturer's instructions. The same butterfly in different colors is used on the butterfly and ladybug sampler. Small butterflies from this chart have been used on the country sampler on page 37, but this time stitched in German flower thread.

*DMC	ANCHOR	PATERNA
798	0941	541
809	0129	545
321	019	951
758	0337	954
938	0381	430
712	0387	261
722	0323	803
327	0872	321
304	047	950
350	011	842
352	09	843
353	06	845
840	0393	462

*GFT	DMC	ANCHOR	PATERNA
2068	335	038	942
2021	3326	026	945
1821	211	0342	322
3512	640	0393	462
2022	799	0850	513
3332	209	0109	303

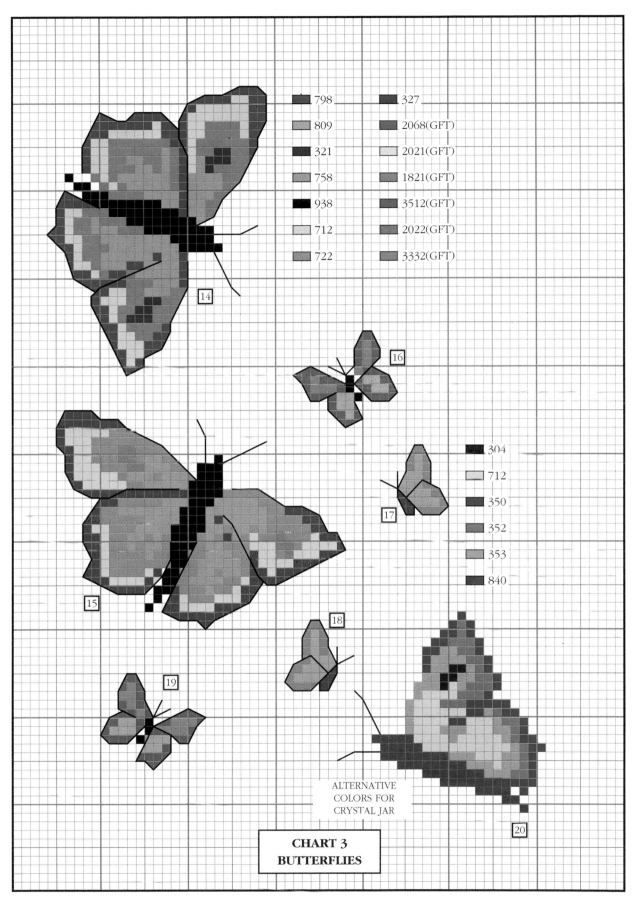

798   327

809   2068(GFT)

321   2021(GFT)

758   1821(GFT)

938   3512(GFT)

712   2022(GFT)

722   3332(GFT)

14

16

304

712

350

352

353

840

17

18

15

19

ALTERNATIVE
COLORS FOR
CRYSTAL JAR

20

**CHART 3
BUTTERFLIES**

CHART 4

BIRDS AND ANIMALS

These charming bird and animal designs have been made into a book cover for James's country diary. The same desings could be used to cover a purchased loose-leaf notebook or scrapbook cover (see Useful Techniques, page 115).

*DMC	ANCHOR	PATERNA
898	0381	460
3032	0392	462
304	047	950
989	0261	613
712	0387	445
561	0218	661
415	0398	212
317	0400	210

CHART 5

*DMC	ANCHOR	PATERNA
632	0379	472
3032	0393	463
301	0349	721
975	0355	402
437	0362	405
301 + 3032	0349 + 0393	721 + 463
3033	0388	454
317	0400	201
415 + 317	0398 + 0400	203 + 201
415	0398	203
561	0218	661
989	0261	613

LEFT:
*Butterfly and ladybug alphabet, James's
country diary, silk thread file, and crystal jar*

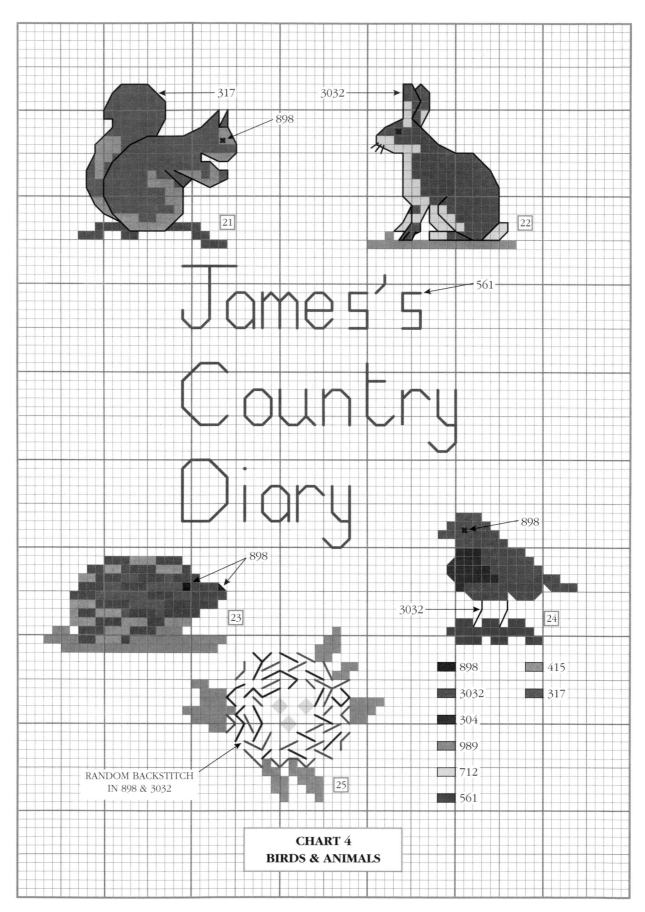

317

3032

898

21

22

James's
Country
Diary

561

898

898

3032

23

24

RANDOM BACKSTITCH
IN 898 & 3032

25

	898		415
	3032		317
	304		
	989		
	712		
	561		

**CHART 4
BIRDS & ANIMALS**

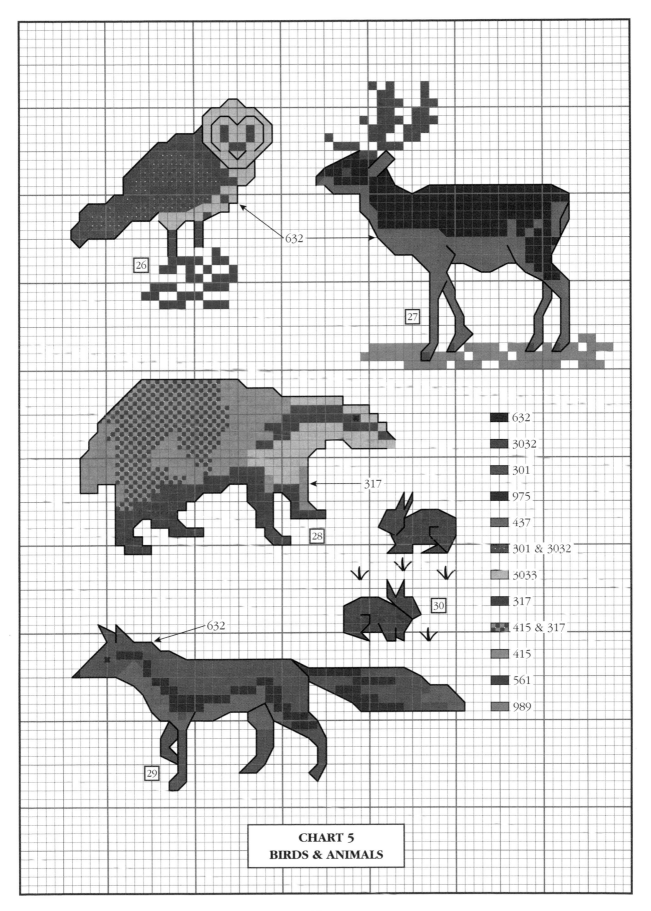

632

26

632

27

317

28

632

29

30

632
3032
301
975
437
301 & 3032
3033
317
415 & 317
415
561
989

CHART 5
BIRDS & ANIMALS

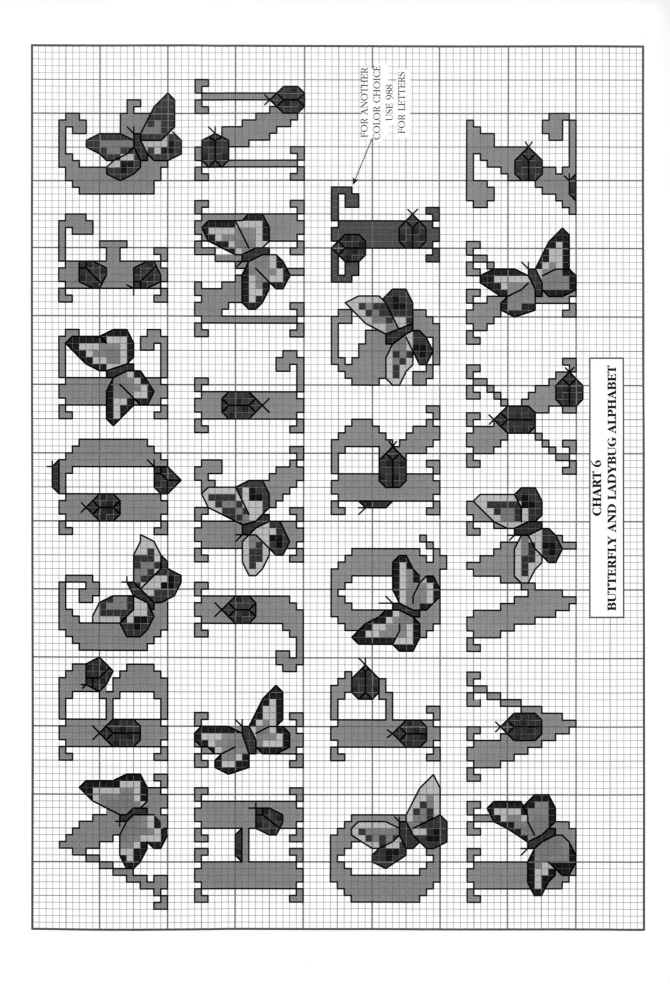

FOR ANOTHER COLOR CHOICE USE 988 FOR LETTERS

CHART 6
BUTTERFLY AND LADYBUG ALPHABET

BUTTERFLY AND LADYBUG ALPHABET

This pretty sampler is made of letters decorated with butterflies and ladybugs (chart 6, key on chart 7) and additional butterflies from chart 3 (page 15).

CHARTS 6 and 7

ALPHABET & BACHELOR'S BUTTON

*DMC	ANCHOR	PATERNA
320	0261	613
349	046	951
722	0323	854
3346	0267	621
327	0872	321
842	0378	472
712	0387	475
(310) BLACK	0403	220
792	0133	550
839	0936	471
809	0129	553

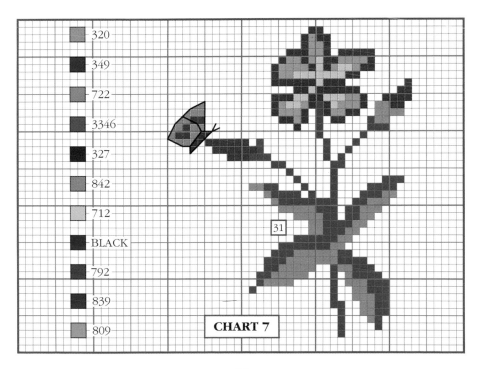

320
349
722
3346
327
842
712
BLACK
792
839
809

CHART 7

CHART 8

HARVEST AND HEDGE MOTIFS

The silk thread file on page 16 is stitched using the same letters as the butterfly alphabet, but adding a poppy, bachelor's button, harvest mouse, or dandelion to the letters. The whole alphabet could be stitched by tracing the letters from page 20 and adding the new motifs as shown.

*DMC	ANCHOR	PATERNA
834	0305	753
793	0123	544
936	0846	600
3347	0843	603
420	0375	434
(310) BLACK	0403	220
304	047	950
WHITE	01	260

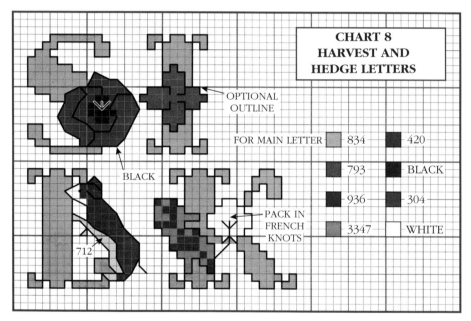

CHART 8 HARVEST AND HEDGE LETTERS

OPTIONAL OUTLINE

BLACK

712

FOR MAIN LETTER

PACK IN FRENCH KNOTS

	834		420
	793		BLACK
	936		304
	3347		WHITE

CHART 9

HARVEST POSY

*DMC	ANCHOR	PATERNA
816	020	840
321	047	950
743	0298	726
437	0362	753
840	0379	472
3347	0843	603
936	0846	600
(310) BLACK	0403	220
793	0123	544
712	0387	327

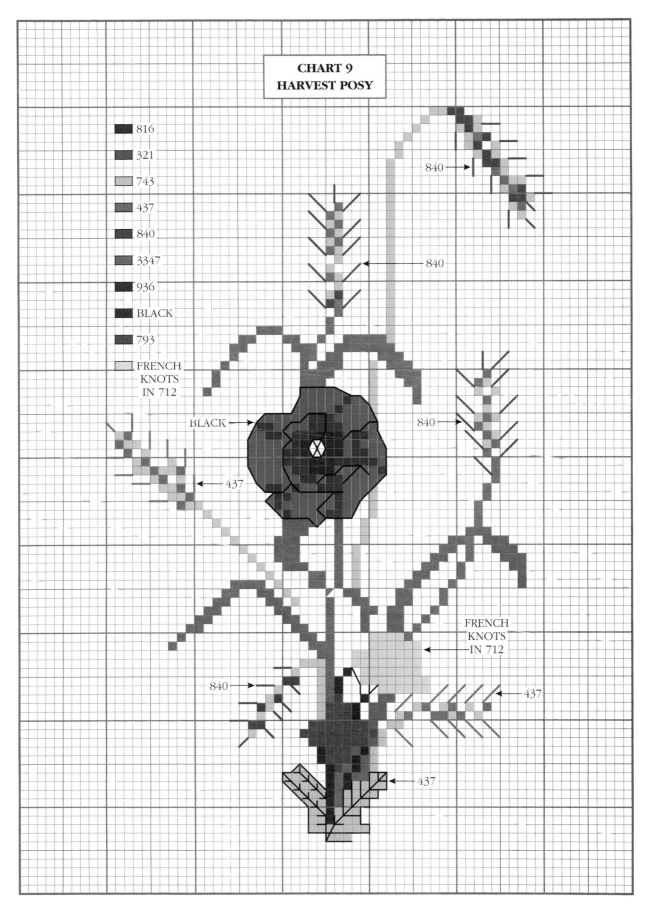

CHART 9
HARVEST POSY

816
321
743
437
840
3347
936
BLACK
793
FRENCH KNOTS IN 712

BLACK

437

840

840

840

FRENCH KNOTS IN 712

840

437

437

Flowers and Alphabets

Flowers are probably the most popular subjects in counted needlework and can be used to decorate clothes, furnishings, and all sorts of other objects.

The designs charted on pages 27 and 29 have been stitched on a plain black vest, and an Afghan throw, and used in the purchased brush and comb set, all illustrated opposite. The vest was cut out from a standard dressmaker's pattern and the flowers stitched before the vest was completed. The brush and comb set was stitched on linen and finished as directed by the manufacturer. The throw was stitched on Afghan fabric using alternate squares (see Fig. 1) and then the edge fringed to a row of machine stitching.

As with many of the designs in this book, the outlines shown on the chart are not always necessary, so work the cross stitch first and then decide how much definition is required.

A		B		E	
	D		C		F
C		F		A	
	B		E		D
E		D		C	
	F		A		B

Fig. 1 Afghan throw

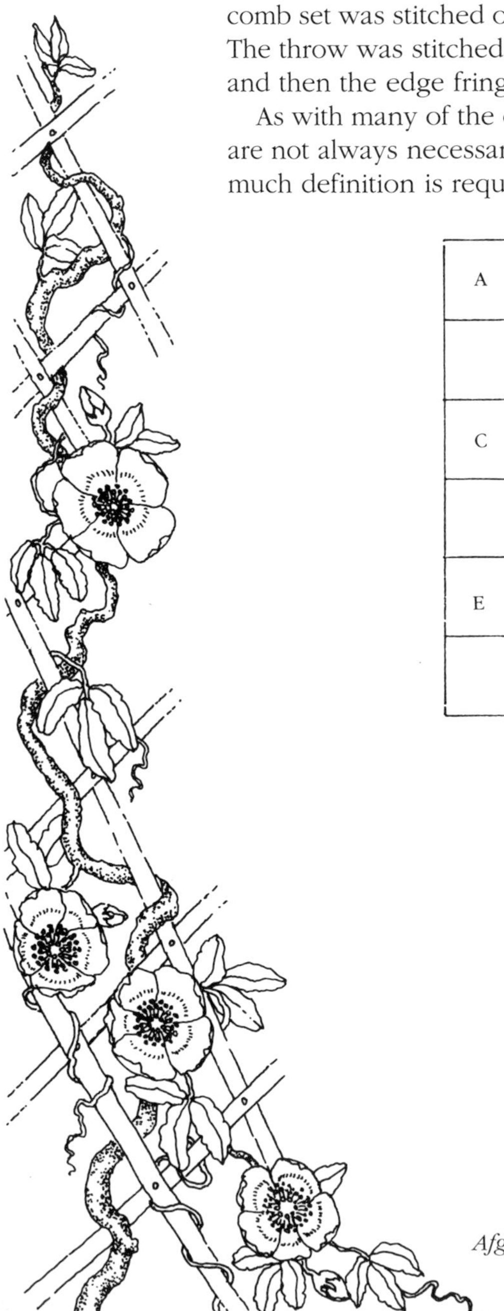

RIGHT:
*Afghan throw, brush and comb set, and
embroidered vest*

CHART 10

SMALL FLOWERS AND POSIES

The small violets (motifs 34 and 35) are ideal designs for small projects like jewelry and trinket pots. The single red rosebud (motif 38) has been used as a corner motif on the rosebud pillow on page 69.

*DMC	ANCHOR	PATERNA
550	0102	310
988	0210	613
937	0263	610
224	0894	914
340	0118	561
809	0129	563
341	0117	564
727	0301	704
3350	0896	912
223	0895	913
470	0281	693
3685	0897	910
939	0152	570
552	0112	311
327	0872	312

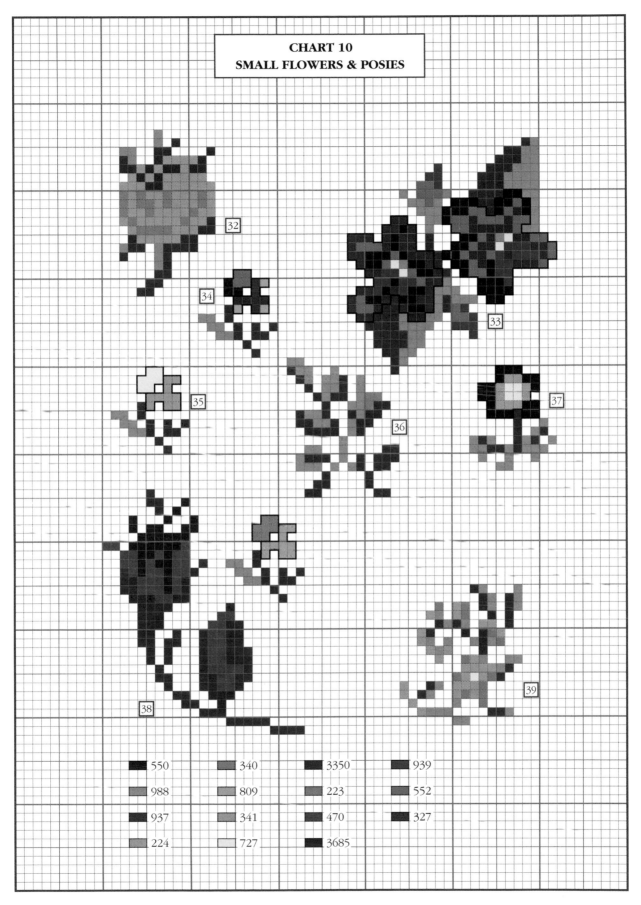

CHART 10
SMALL FLOWERS & POSIES

	550		340		3350		939
	988		809		223		552
	937		341		470		327
	224		727		3685		

CHART 11

LARGE FLOWERS AND POSIES

*DMC	ANCHOR	PATERNA
224	0894	914
939	0152	570
340	0118	561
352	09	843
3350	0896	912
758	0337	845
988	0262	612
3350 + 3685	0896 + 0897	912 + 910
223	0895	913
351	010	845
989	0261	612
937	0263	610
727	0301	714
891	035	843
341	0117	561
792	0123	560
712	0387	756

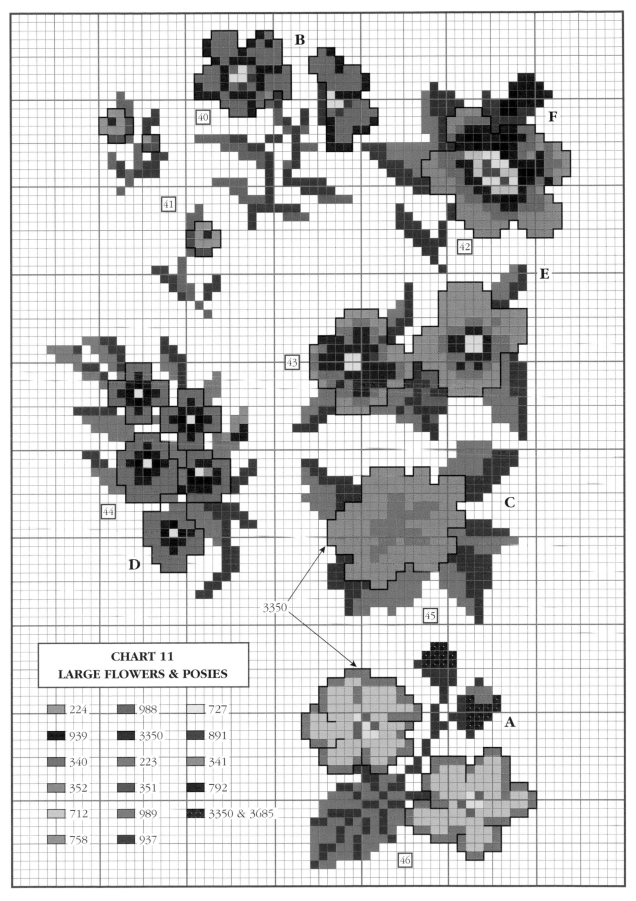

B

F

40

41

42

E

43

44

C

D

3350

45

CHART 11
LARGE FLOWERS & POSIES

	224		988		727
	939		3350		891
	340		223		341
	352		351		792
	712		989		3350 & 3685
	758		937		

A

46

FLOWER ALPHABET

This charming colorful alphabet has been stitched in two color choices to demonstrate how versatile it can be. It is charted over four pages in green and pink, with one letter shown in the dark blue version (chart 15B). These decorated letters are useful for adding initials to greeting cards or to a special gift.

The picture of the recipe folder and my daughter's name plate (opposite) illustrates just how different this alphabet can look when alternative fabrics and threads are chosen. Both designs were stitched in stranded floss, using two strands for the cross stitch. The outline illustrated on the chart is optional and could be worked in one strand of floss in a contrasting color.

CHARTS 12, 13, 14, 15A

*DMC	ANCHOR	PATERNA
562	0216	1009
223	0895	1002
3350	0896	2088
727	0295	1049
712	0387	1001

CHART 15B

*DMC	ANCHOR	PATERNA
939	0152	3022
894	075	1002
602	063	2088
600	039	1105
727	0295	2084
712	0387	1001

RIGHT:
Recipe folder and Louise name plate

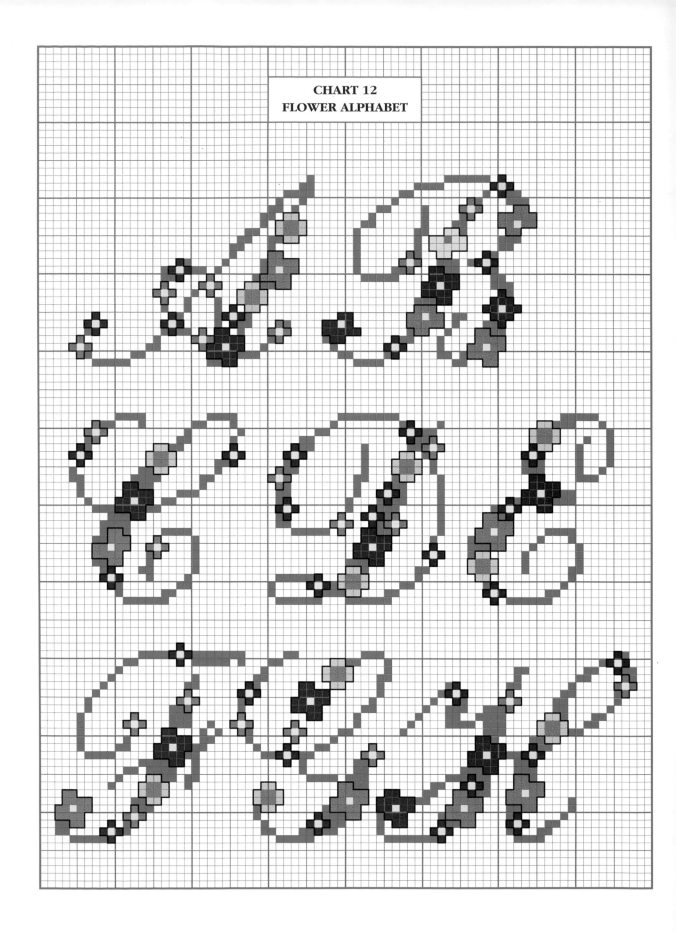

CHART 12
FLOWER ALPHABET

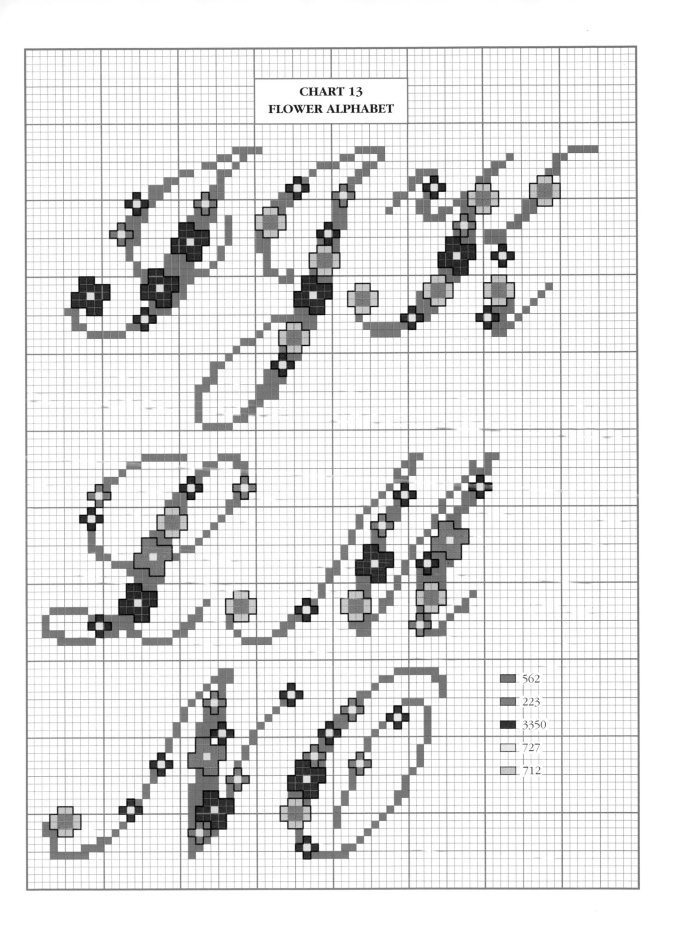

CHART 13
FLOWER ALPHABET

562
223
3350
727
712

CHART 14
FLOWER ALPHABET

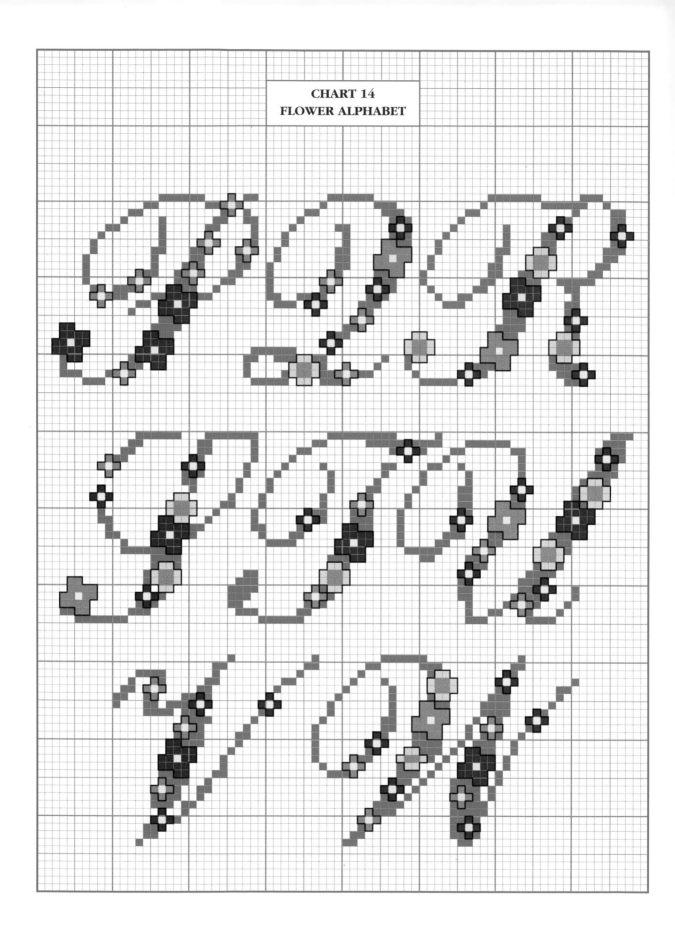

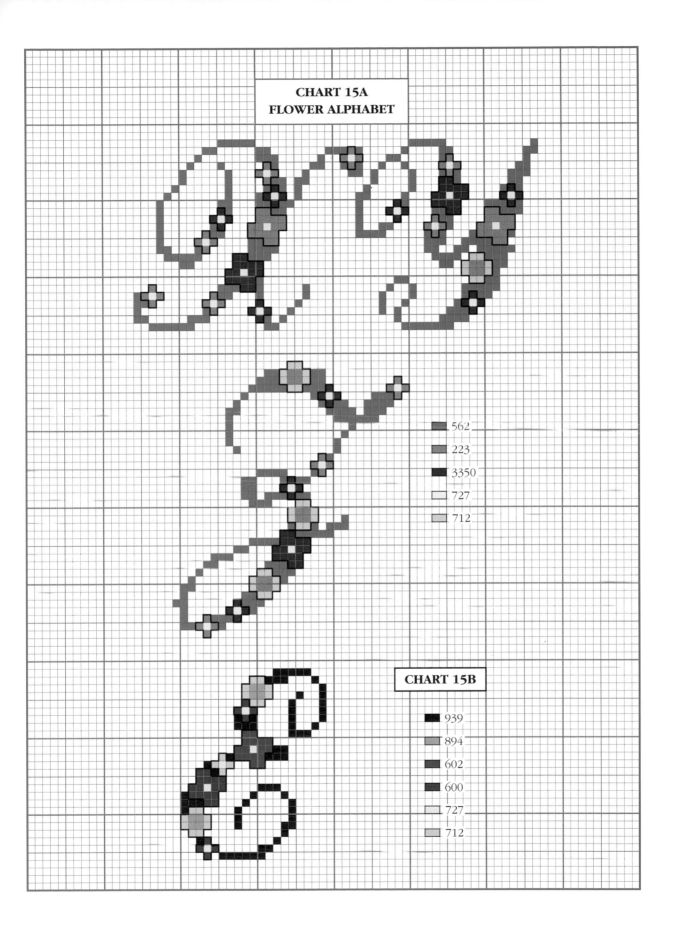

CHART 15A
FLOWER ALPHABET

■	562
■	223
■	3350
▢	727
▨	712

CHART 15B

■	939
■	894
■	602
■	600
▢	727
▨	712

Samplers

THE COUNTRY SAMPLER

This pretty traditional sampler was stitched using a single strand of German flower thread on linen. The picture (opposite) combines border no. 1, the alphabet from chart 17, and butterflies, bird's nest, and rabbits from charts 3, 4, and 5. The small amount of outline was added using one strand of floss in DMC shade 317. French knot roses and stones are added to the house and the outside of the pond after the cross stitch has been completed.

CHARTS 16A and B

*GFT	DMC	ANCHOR
3112	937	0263
2081	340	0118
3822	932	0850
3001	320	0261
2088	3350	0896
2068	223	0895
1821	3608	970
1600	433	0357
1007	640	0393
2052	605	074
2096	351	010
2000	471	0265
3332	327	0872
1000	712	0387
1222	738	0372
2011	552	0112
3022	BLACK	0403
	317	0400

RIGHT:
The country sampler

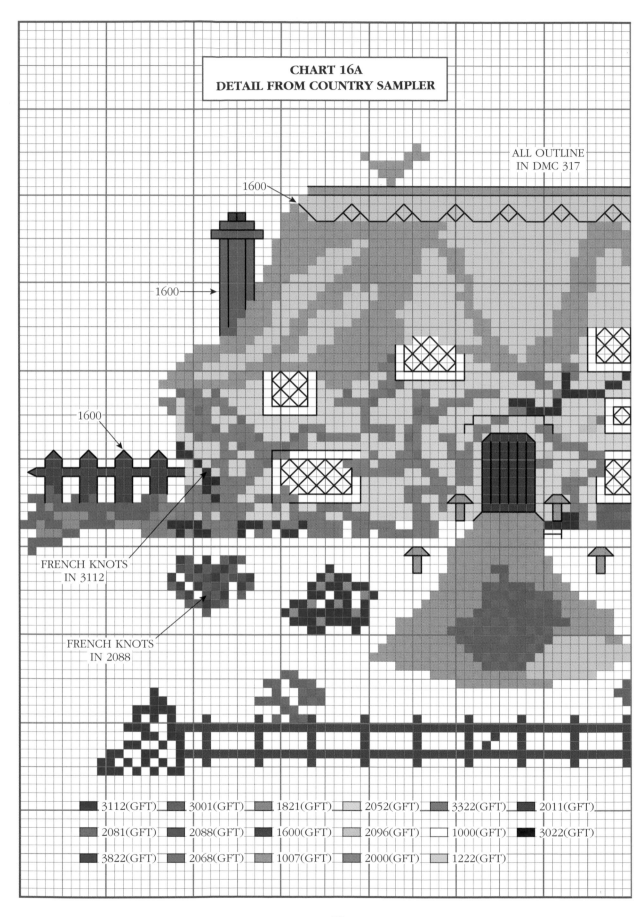

**CHART 16A
DETAIL FROM COUNTRY SAMPLER**

ALL OUTLINE
IN DMC 317

1600

1600

1600

FRENCH KNOTS
IN 3112

FRENCH KNOTS
IN 2088

3112(GFT)	3001(GFT)	1821(GFT)	2052(GFT)	3322(GFT)	2011(GFT)
2081(GFT)	2088(GFT)	1600(GFT)	2096(GFT)	1000(GFT)	3022(GFT)
3822(GFT)	2068(GFT)	1007(GFT)	2000(GFT)	1222(GFT)	

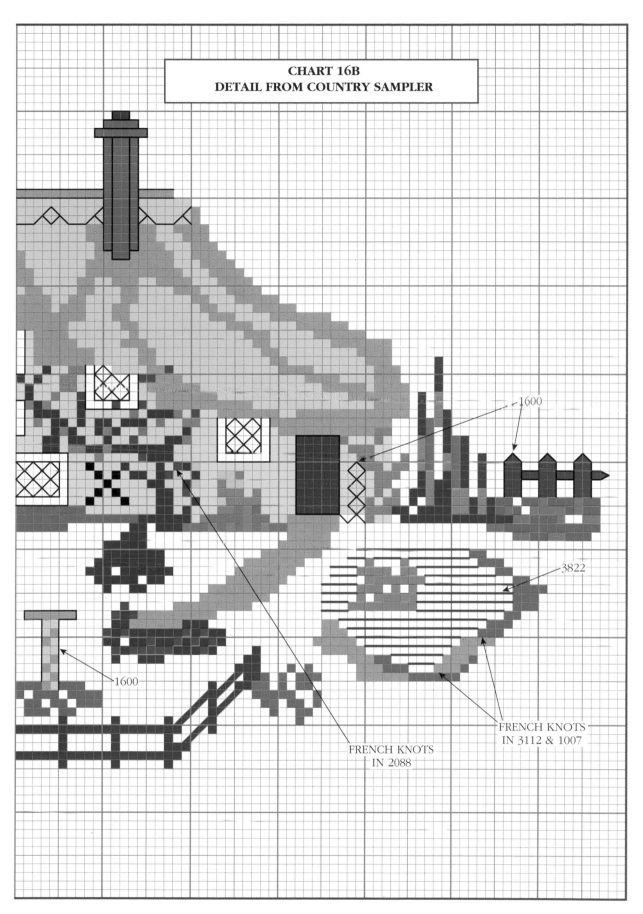

CHART 16B
DETAIL FROM COUNTRY SAMPLER

1600

3822

1600

FRENCH KNOTS
IN 3112 & 1007

FRENCH KNOTS
IN 2088

LITTLE ALPHABET AND TREE SAMPLER

The alphabet in the tree sampler opposite was taken from a design stitched in 1850. The tree sampler is an adaption of the theme of Adam and Eve often used by Victorian needlewomen. It uses border 13 (page 13), baskets of fruit from chart 28 (page 62), the apple motif from chart 53 (page 112), and the garlands from chart 34 on page 78.

CHART 17

*DMC	ANCHOR	PATERNA
930	0851	512
420	0375	441
738	0372	443
932	0850	513
436	0373	442

CHART 18

*DMC	ANCHOR	PATERNA
433	0357	471
502	0876	D546
3350	0896	901
501	0878	D556
317	0400	210
727	0295	727
632	0379	472
898	0381	470
223	0895	904
945	0311	886
501	0878	D516

RIGHT:
The tree sampler and the little alphabet

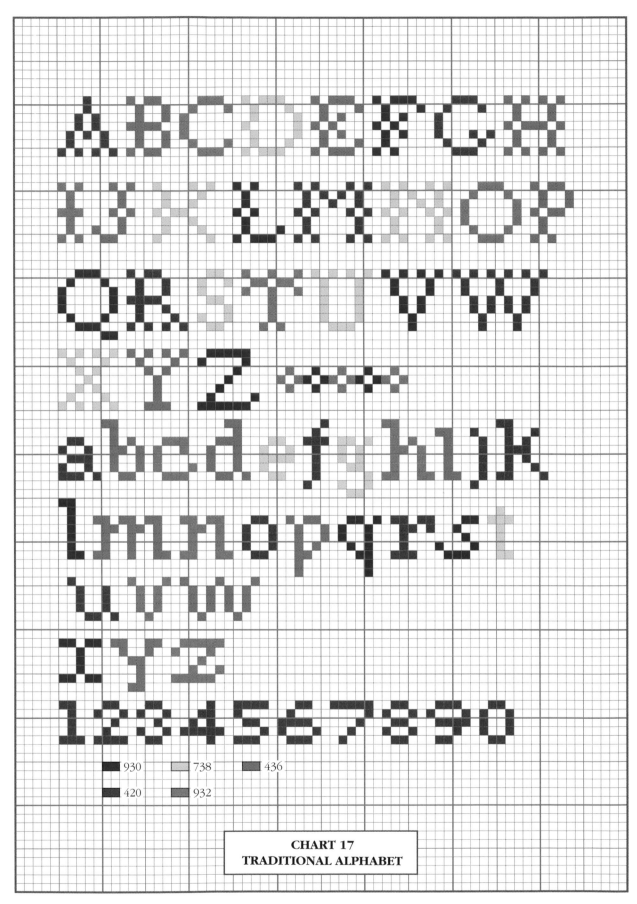

CHART 17
TRADITIONAL ALPHABET

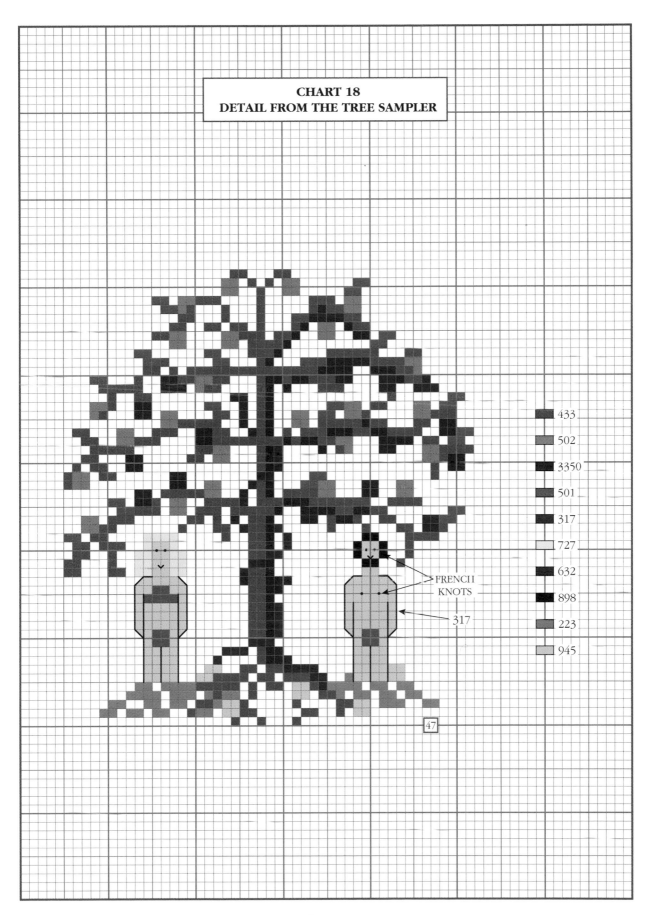

CHART 18
DETAIL FROM THE TREE SAMPLER

433
502
3350
501
317
727
632
898
223
945

FRENCH
KNOTS

317

47

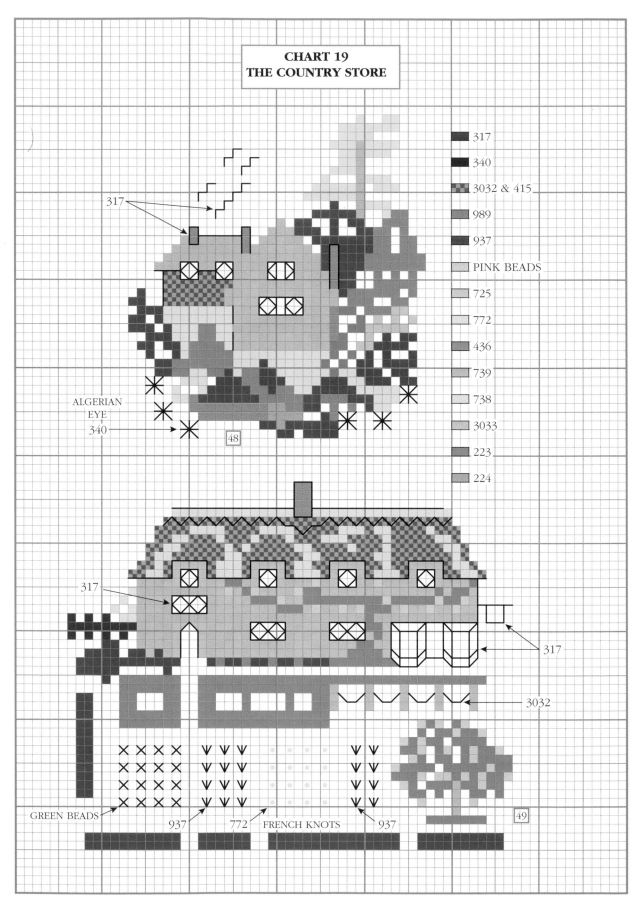

CHART 19
THE COUNTRY STORE

317

340

3032 & 415

989

937

PINK BEADS

725

772

436

739

738

3033

223

224

317

ALGERIAN
EYE
340

48

317

317

3032

GREEN BEADS

937   772   FRENCH KNOTS   937

49

An English Village

The picture on pages 50–51 is a lovely design, combining cottages, the church, the village pub, the country store, and even the village stocks, all surrounded by border 10 from chart 2 (page 13). They are stitched in stranded floss, and a few glass beads are used for added interest. The cross stitch is worked using two strands of floss, the outline in one strand of dark gray, and the beads attached with a half cross stitch and one strand of matching thread. The Algerian eye is stitched using two strands of floss (see Fig. 2 on page 49) and can be seen in the illustration pages 50–51.

THE COUNTRY STORE
CHART 19

*DMC	ANCHOR	PATERNA
340	0118	343
3032 + 415	0392 + 0398	463 + 203
989	0261	613
937	0263	610
725	0306	703
772	0259	614
436	0373	752
739	0361	755
738	0372	754
3033	0388	645
223	0895	913
224	0894	914
317	0400	200

THE VILLAGE CHURCH
CHART 20

*DMC	ANCHOR	PATERNA
937	0263	610
304	047	950
772	0259	695
834	0874	753
640	0393	462
3032	0392	463
3033	0388	465
415 + 317	0398 + 0400	203 + 200
436	0373	442
437 + 738	0362 + 0372	445 + 444
738	0372	444
898	0381	471
989	0261	613
317	0400	200

45

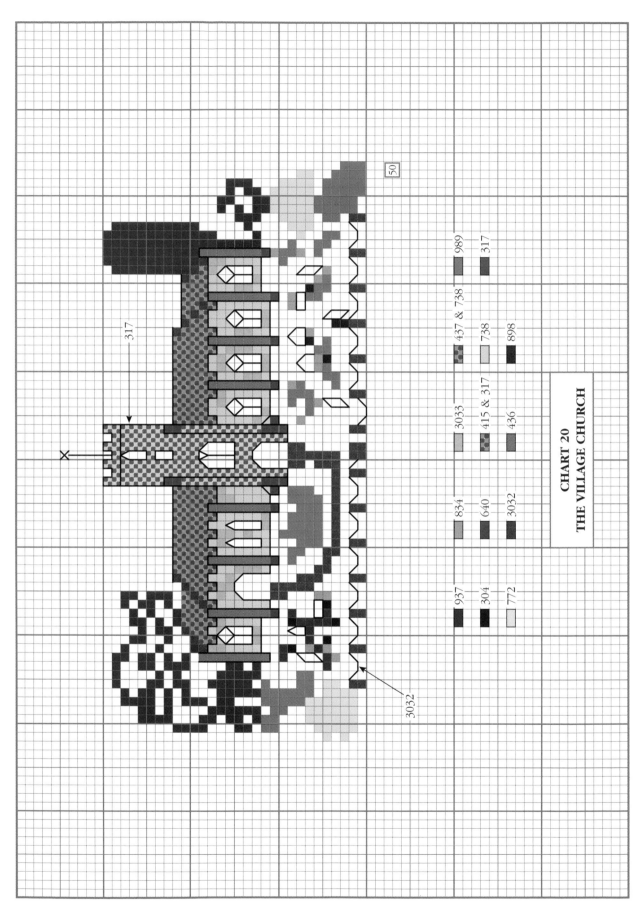

CHART 20
THE VILLAGE CHURCH

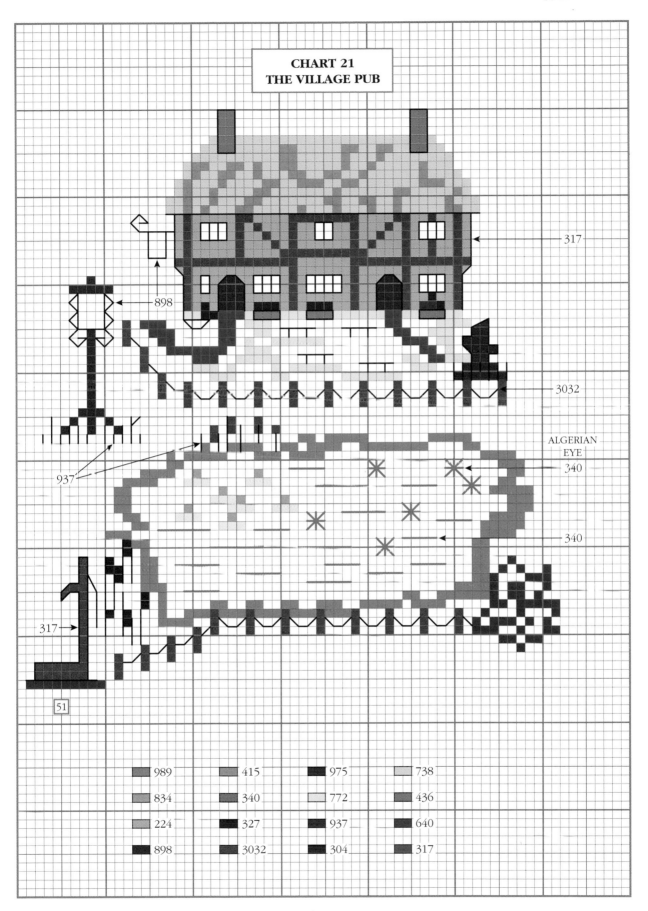

CHART 21
THE VILLAGE PUB

317

898

3032

ALGERIAN
EYE
340

340

937

317

51

■ 989	■ 415	■ 975	■ 738
■ 834	■ 340	■ 772	■ 436
■ 224	■ 327	■ 937	■ 640
■ 898	■ 3032	■ 304	■ 317

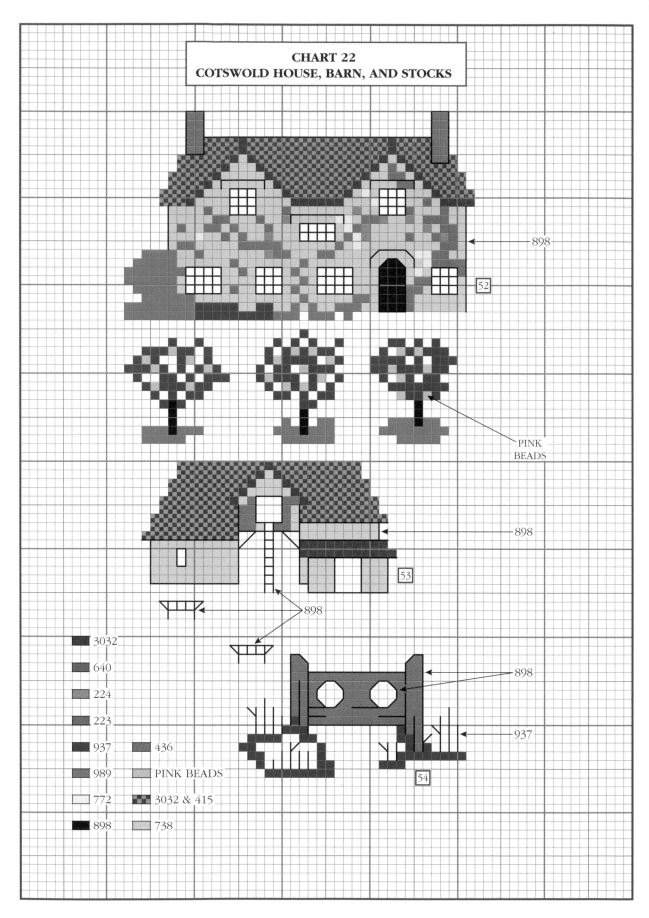

CHART 22
COTSWOLD HOUSE, BARN, AND STOCKS

898

52

PINK
BEADS

898

53

898

898

937

54

3032	
640	
224	
223	
937	436
989	PINK BEADS
772	3032 & 415
898	738

THE VILLAGE PUB, COTSWOLD HOUSE, BARN, AND STOCKS

This pretty pub is stitched in a soft shade of pink rather like the plastered buildings in some rural areas of England. The pond in the foreground is decorated in small beads to represent water plants; the rushes around the edge could be worked in cross stitch or French knots, or you could add beads.

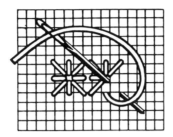

Fig. 2 Algerian eye (see chart 21)

The technique of mixing colors together to create a mottled effect is well illustrated here. It is particularly effective in the roof of the Cotswold house.

CHARTS 21 and 22

*DMC	ANCHOR	PATERNA
989	0261	612
834	0874	753
224	0894	932
898	0381	470
415	0398	202
340	0118	343
327	0872	321
3032	0392	463
975	0355	402
772	0259	614
937	0263	611
304	047	970
738	0372	444
436	0373	443
640	0393	462
317	0400	210
223	0895	933

PAGES 50–51
The English village sampler and tree picture

The Country Kitchen

BREAD, ROLLS, AND HARVEST MOTIF

One of the most evocative images of living in the country is probably the farmhouse kitchen, complete with range and a scrubbed pine table covered with homemade preserves, pickles, and – best of all – crusty home-baked bread.

The bread bag illustrated on pages 58–59 was inspired by a visit to Germany where bread is brought home in purchased or homemade "Brot" bags, and the bag is simply washed in the washing machine as necessary. The roll cover pictured uses some of the bread motifs on one corner, a theme which could be extended to other things, such as napkins.

CHART 23

*DMC	ANCHOR
898	0381
436	0373
725	0306
738	0372
304	047
420	0375
309	042
930	0851
BLACK	0403

MAKING BAGS

All the bags illustrated in this book are made in basically the same way. When the embroidery is completed, the design is pressed on the wrong side. Then place the right sides of the material together and stitch the edges by hand or machine (see Fig. 3). The bread bag is lined with washable polyester and cotton fabric and includes a casing for the drawstring.

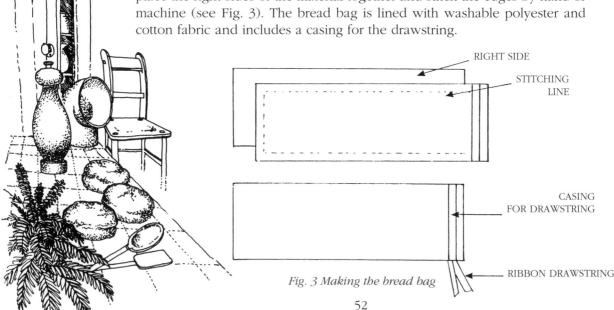

RIGHT SIDE

STITCHING LINE

CASING FOR DRAWSTRING

RIBBON DRAWSTRING

Fig. 3 Making the bread bag

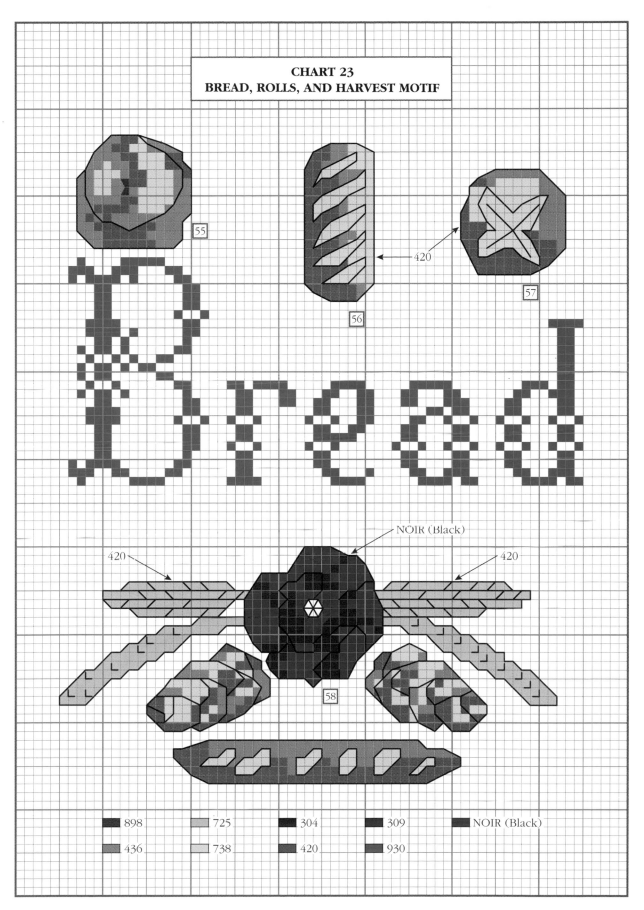

CHART 23
BREAD, ROLLS, AND HARVEST MOTIF

55

420

57

56

NOIR (Black)

420

420

58

| | 898 | | 725 | | 304 | | 309 | | NOIR (Black) |
| | 436 | | 738 | | 420 | | 930 | | |

CONDIMENTS

On this chart, familiar kitchen images have been devised to make simple projects to decorate a shelf or even part of a hamper intended as a gift. Any or all of these motifs could be combined with great effect to make a kitchen sampler. Motifs 60 and 61 have been made into bags for kitchen staples, and the blue casserole dish has been included in the oven mitt illustrated on page 59.

All the designs on this chart were stitched in stranded floss, using two strands for the cross stitch and one strand for the outlining.

CHART 24

*DMC	ANCHOR	*DMC	ANCHOR
420	0375	3033	0388
738	0372	640	0393
436	0373	340	0118
930	0851	341	0117
WHITE	01	797	0133

CHART 25

This simple chart provides the lettering for projects such as the magnetic fridge noteboard (page 65) and the message board (pages 8–9). The message board (which comes complete with manufacturer's finishing instructions) is stitched on Aida in stranded floss using borders 4, 5, and 6 from page 11. It has the days of the week and a place to list "things to do."

WINE BAG AND COFFEE MUG

The simple wine bag illustrated on pages 58–59 has been made as a drawstring bag, but it could easily be adapted and by adding a pair of handles it can be used to carry a bottle to a party! The coffee mug has been designed especially for cross stitch, and comes complete with scrubbable plastic Aida fabric.

All these designs were stitched in stranded floss, using two strands for the cross stitch and one strand for the outline. The grapes on the coffee mug were stitched using purple with the small grape motif (no. 63). The apple apron is a purchased linen apron with the cross-stitched apple motif from chart 53 (page 112) in three strands of floss.

CHART 26

*DMC	ANCHOR	GFT
937	0263	3702
327	0872	2011
472	0278	2099
554	0109	2011
471	0279	3732
611	0832	5312

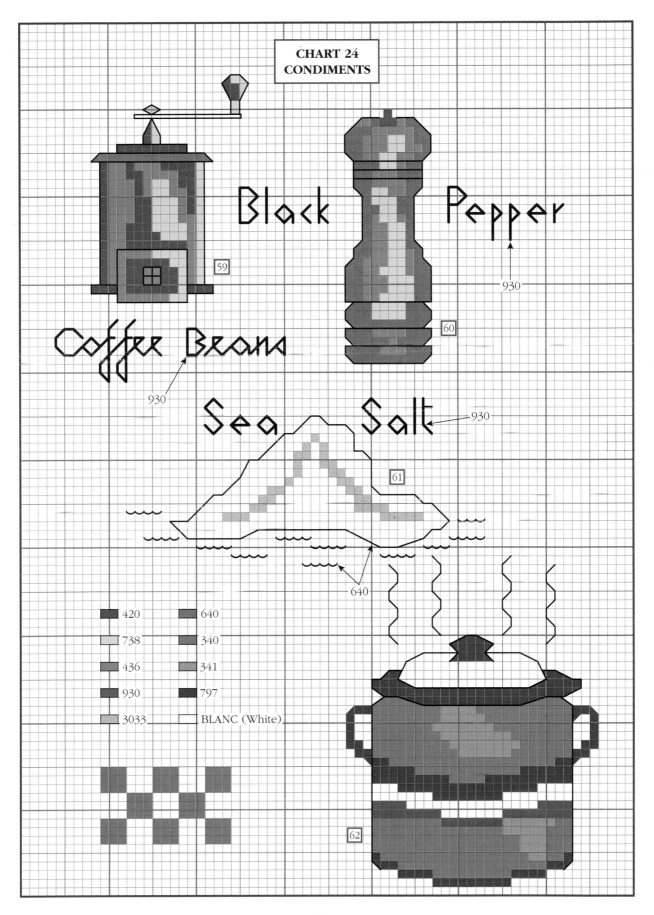

**CHART 24
CONDIMENTS**

Black Pepper

59

Coffee Beans

930

60

930

Sea Salt

930

61

640

	420		640
	738		340
	436		341
	930		797
	3033		BLANC (White)

62

CHART 25
LETTERING CHART

Sun   Thur

Mon   Fri

Tue   Sat

Wed   Things to do

Forget-me-not

Jan   June   Nov

Feb   July   Dec

March   August

April   Sept

May   Oct

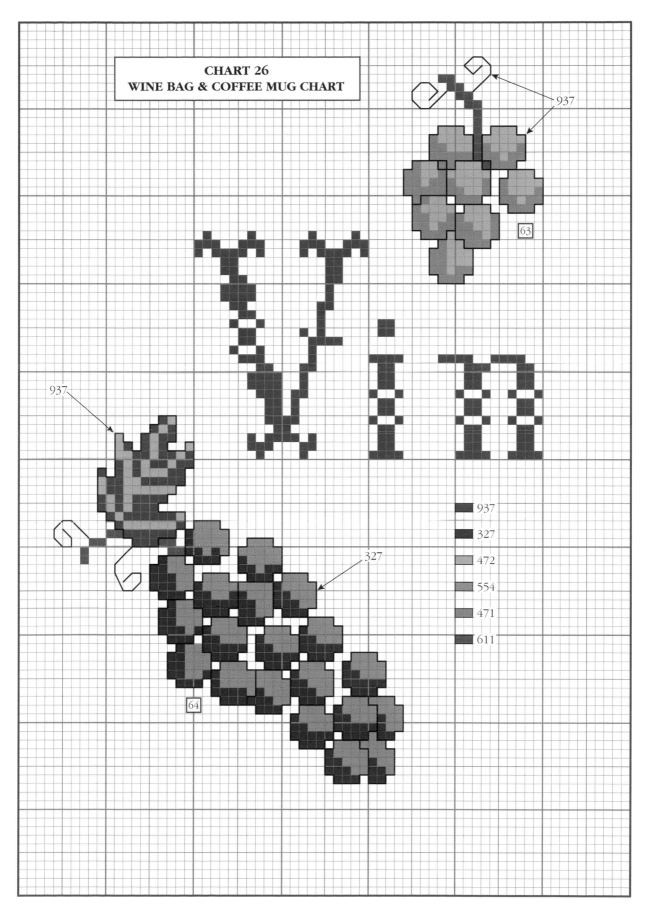

CHART 26
WINE BAG & COFFEE MUG CHART

937

63

937

327

937
327
472
554
471
611

64

Clockwise from top left:
*Bread bag, mitten, bag for peppercorns, coffee mug,
bag for sea salt, roll cover (folded beneath
coffee mug), apple apron (beneath roll
cover), bag for wine bottle, bag for coffee*

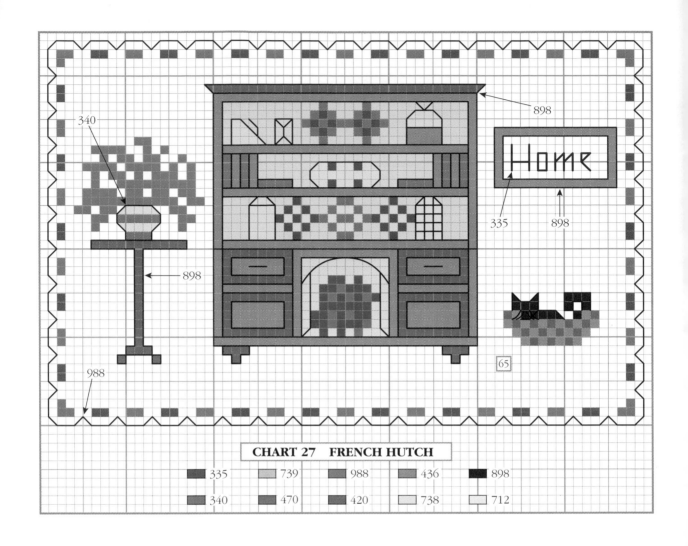

CHART 27   FRENCH HUTCH

▨ 335	▨ 739	▨ 988	▨ 436	▨ 898
▨ 340	▨ 470	▨ 420	▨ 738	▨ 712

FRENCH HUTCH

A French hutch with a full display of china is a popular image from a farmhouse kitchen, possibly as popular as the range. This simple design has been made as a lovely card which could very well be framed.

The stitched version varies slightly from the chart to make sure the correct balance was achieved on the purchased card. Again, this motif would be ideal as part of a design for a kitchen sampler.

CHART 27

*DMC	ANCHOR
335	041
340	0118
739	0366
470	0281
988	0262
420	0375
436	0373
738	0372
898	0381
712	0387

CHART 28
BASKETS OF FRUIT

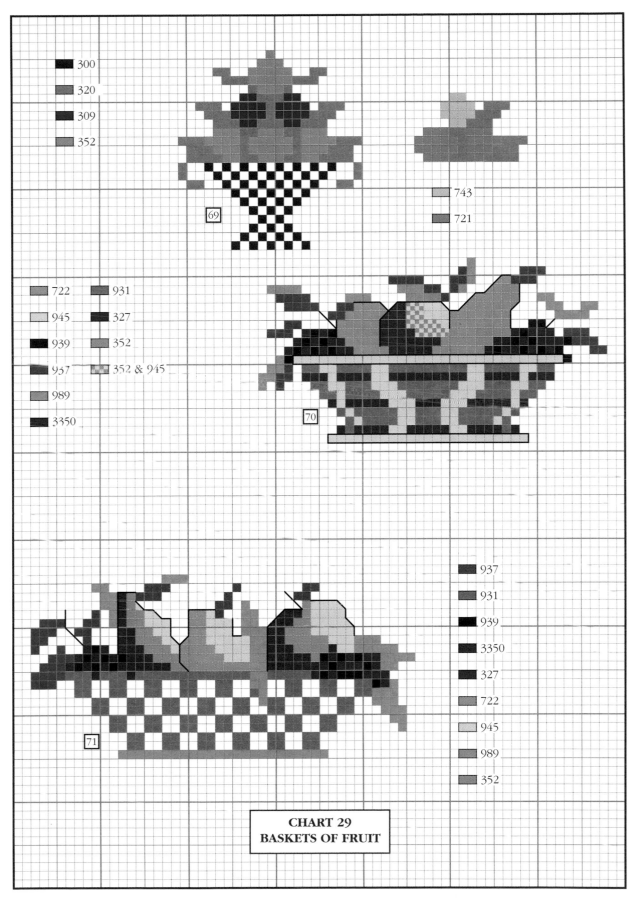

300
320
309
352

69

743
721

722   931
945   327
939   352
957   352 & 945
989
3350

70

937
931
939
3350
327
722
945
989
352

71

CHART 29
BASKETS OF FRUIT

BASKETS OF FRUIT

These lovely designs originated in Germany in the 1930s, yet they still look modern and fresh today. The picture on page 65 shows two of the baskets (motifs 70 and 71) made as small recipe holders; also preserve labels, which use motif 69; and a magnetic fridge noteboard using motif 68. Motif 66 is used as part of the tree sampler design illustrated on page 41. The clock is designed using motif 71 surrounded with random apples in matching colors, then made according to the manufacturer's instructions.

CHART 28

*DMC	ANCHOR	PATERNA
501	0878	521
3350	0896	902
939	0152	570
503	0875	522
327	0872	321
632	0379	472
898	0381	430
966	0214	664
223	0895	905
224	0894	904
3685	0897	901
562	0216	662
433	0357	432
436	0373	435
738	0372	436

CHART 29

*DMC	ANCHOR	PATERNA
300	0357	402
320	0261	613
309	042	941
352	09	863
743	0301	704
721	0324	802
722	0323	803
945	06	865
939	0152	570
937	0263	611
989	0262	612
3350	0896	902
931	0921	562
327	0872	321
352 + 945	09 + 06	863 + 865

RIGHT:
Basket-of-fruit, gingham-bordered recipe holders and framed pictures, preserve labels, magnetic fridge noteboard, and clock

Wreaths and Garlands

CHRISTMAS ROSE PILLOW

This gorgeous rose wreath was inspired by a painting seen in Germany. The design is stitched on linen in stranded floss, using two strands for the cross stitch and one for the outlining; the worked piece was then made into this lovely pillow, a fitting partner to the rosebud pillow – both illustrated overleaf. The Christmas rose seen on each corner of the pillow in the photograph is the single rose on the chart, reversed to fit.

The wreath was also stitched on Aida with the ribbons seen in chart 54 (motif 109) added, and the piece was set in the tray illustrated on pages 8–9 and page 69.

CHART 30

*DMC	ANCHOR	PATERNA
937	0263	611
502	0876	662
562	0216	621
472	0278	671
727	0301	704
ECRU	0388	755
415	0398	202
712	0387	655
772	0259	614
792	0123	560
340	0118	562
471	0279	673
680	0901	732
725	0306	726
3350	0896	902
3685	0897	901
936	0846	601
224	0894	904
501	0878	661

PAGES 68–69
*Christmas rose pillow and round tray,
rosebud pillow, and wooden trinket box*

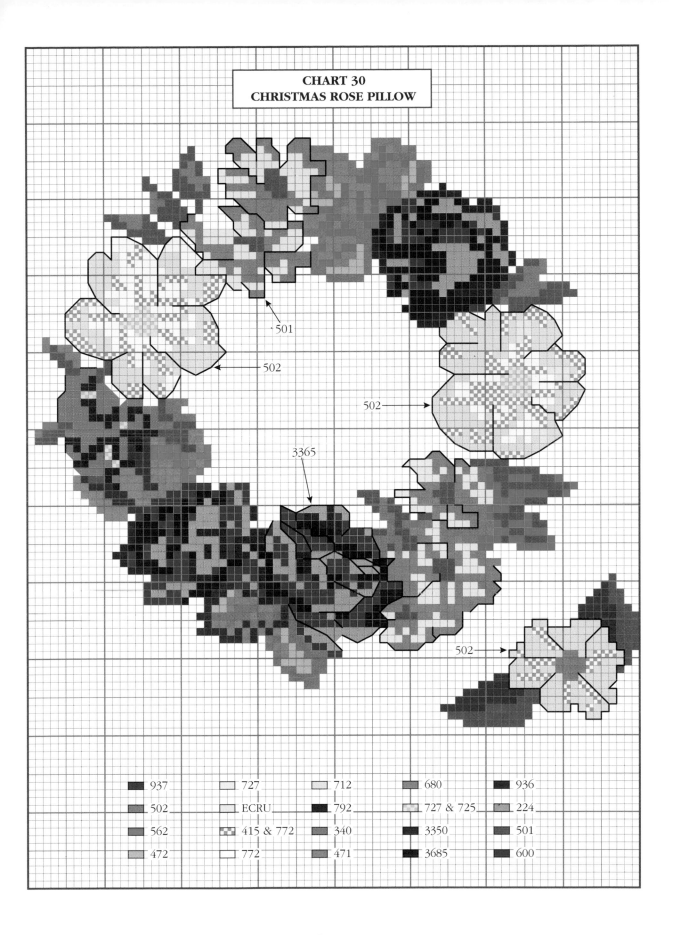

CHART 30
CHRISTMAS ROSE PILLOW

501
502
502
3365
502

937	727	712	680	936
502	ECRU	792	727 & 725	224
562	415 & 772	340	3350	501
472	772	471	3685	600

ROSEBUD PILLOW

This Victorian garland, discovered on an old footstool, was probably based on a Berlin woolwork chart. Here, it has been stitched on linen in stranded floss, using two strands for the cross stitch and one for the outline.

This design and the Christmas rose on page 67 have been made into pillows to prove just how effective cross stitch can be. The rosebud design was also stitched in stranded floss on fine canvas with a dark blue background supplied by Paterna. Once completed, the canvas was mounted on the top of the wooden trinket box as seen in the pictures on page 8 and page 68.

CHART 31

*DMC	ANCHOR	PATERNA
727	0301	704
680	0901	733
834	0874	663
3685	0897	900
223	0895	903
224	0894	904
433	0357	730
937	0263	601
470	0261	613
320	0262	612
939	0152	570
341	0117	562
792	0123	551

**CHART 31
ROSEBUD PILLOW**

☐ 727	■ 3685	■ 433	■ 320	☐ 341
■ 680	■ 223	■ 937	■ 939	■ 792
■ 834	■ 224	■ 470		

FLOWERS FOR PINCUSHIONS

These two simple motifs have been stitched in stranded floss and made into pincushions as illustrated opposite. The single rose motif no. 72 was combined with the heart-shaped garland on chart 35, motif 77, adding a simple latticework effect with backstitch. If you are making these designs to fit purchased wooden bases, always check the design size with your fabric choice. Once the design is finished, assemble as below.

CHART 32

*DMC	ANCHOR	PATERNA
224	0894	906
3350	0896	902
223	0895	903
937	0263	611
3326	075	944
3687	069	904
761	031	945
989	0262	613

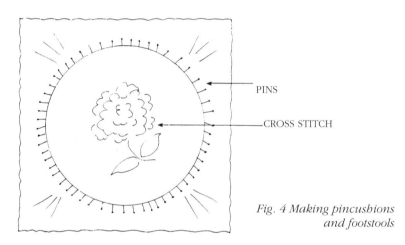

PINS

CROSS STITCH

Fig. 4 Making pincushions and footstools

MAKING PINCUSHIONS AND FOOTSTOOLS

The footstool, pincushions, and the wooden trinket box are all assembled as follows: Press the needlework on the wrong side with a warm iron and set aside. Undo the screw or screws on the bottom of the purchased wooden base and keep them in a safe place. Mark the center of the foam pad and the embroidery with a pin. Match the two points and, smoothing out the material as you go, pin the material to the bottom edge of the pad (see Fig. 4). When you have pinned all the way around, check that there are no folds or puckers to be seen and that the design is in the right place, then lace in position as illustrated in Fig. 7, page 116. Replace the wooden base and screw it into position.

RIGHT;
Footstool and two wooden pincushions

FOOTSTOOL

The design is stitched in German flower thread and DMC stranded floss, worked on unbleached linen, and then made into the lovely footstool illustrated on page 73. If you prefer, the design could be stitched using yarn on canvas. Where possible, the color key lists alternatives, though some of the shades have no equivalent.

CHARTS 33 and 34

*DMC	*GFT	ANCHOR	PATERNA
550	1005	0102	311
939	3022	0152	570
902	3114	045	900
3685	2041	0897	901
335		041	904
601	2073	078	961
352	3311	09	844
729	2082	0891	733
725	2084	0306	726
738	2003	0372	754
712	1001	0387	755
745	2061	0300	727
420	3302	0375	752
832		0907	742
834		0874	743
368	2000	0214	664
500	3702	0224	600
502	3902	0876	602
470	3212	0267	692
369	2001	0265	612
3348	2099	0260	614
677		0305	745
833		0907	753
562	3001	0216	662
783	1932	0307	713
327		0872	321
3041	3432	0109	322
552	2011	0112	311

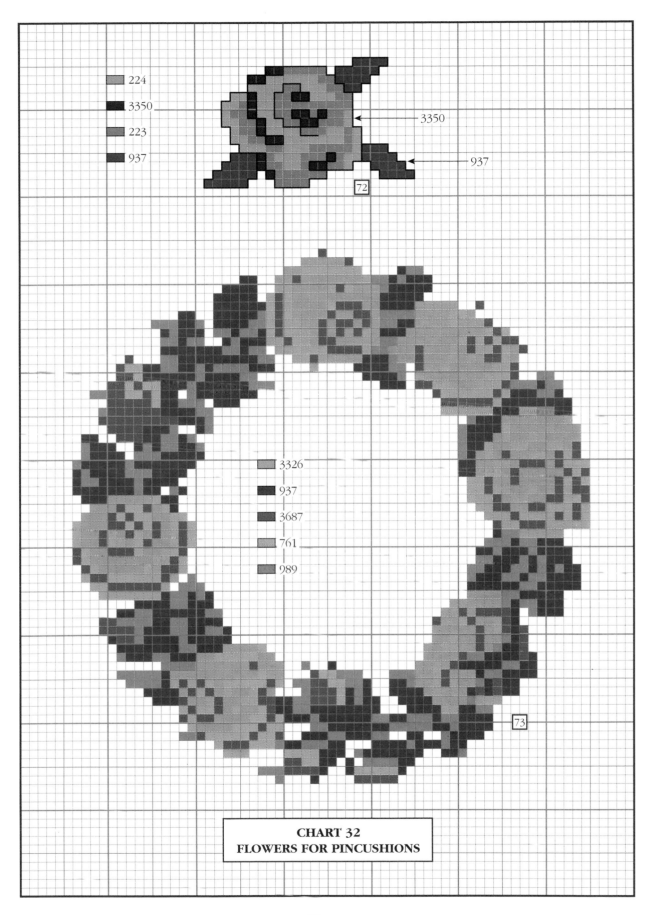

224

3350

223

937

3350

937

72

3326

937

3687

761

989

73

CHART 32
FLOWERS FOR PINCUSHIONS

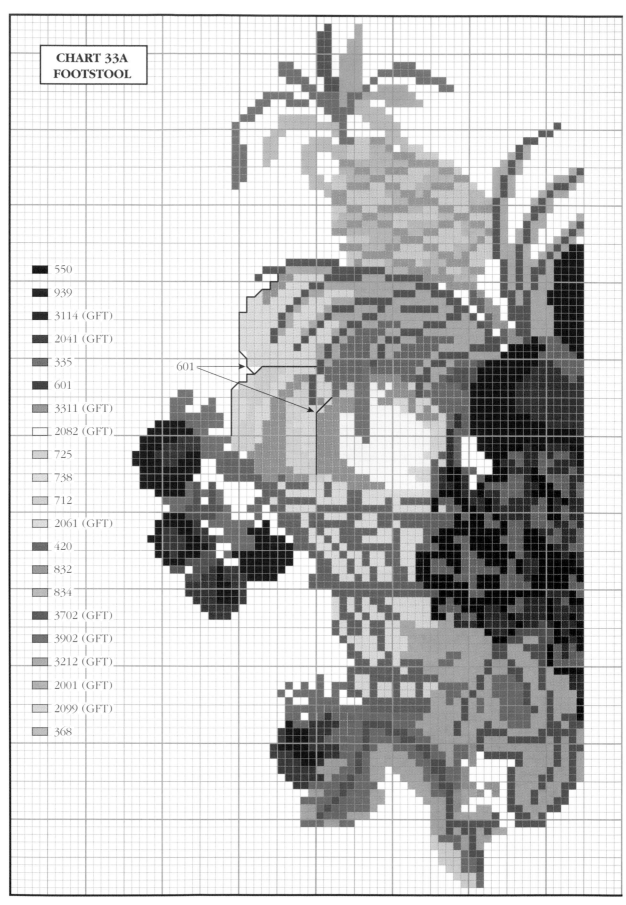

CHART 33A
FOOTSTOOL

550
939
3114 (GFT)
2041 (GFT)
335
601
3311 (GFT)
2082 (GFT)
725
738
712
2061 (GFT)
420
832
834
3702 (GFT)
3902 (GFT)
3212 (GFT)
2001 (GFT)
2099 (GFT)
368

601

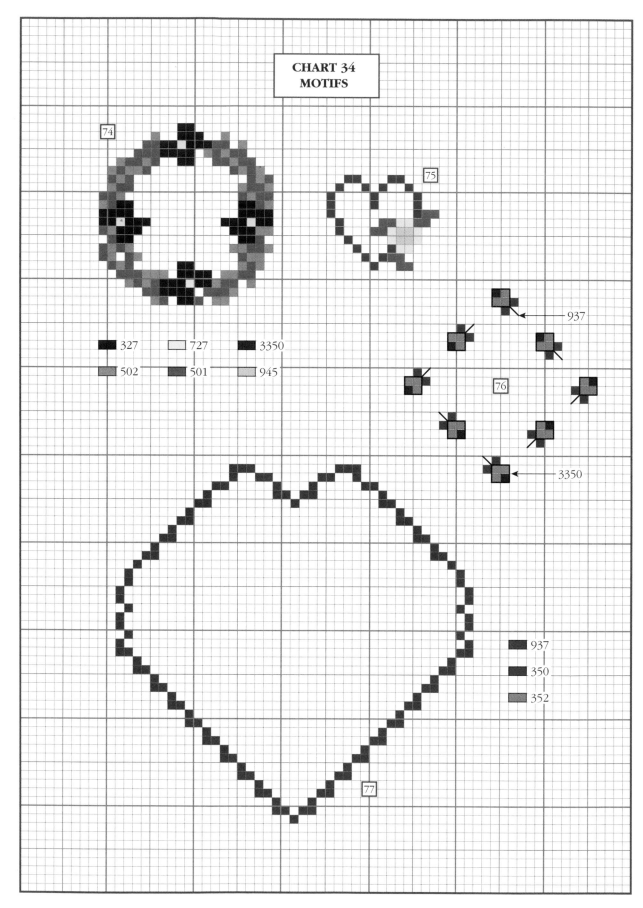

CHART 34
MOTIFS

74

75

327　　727　　3350
502　　501　　945

937

76

3350

937

350

352

77

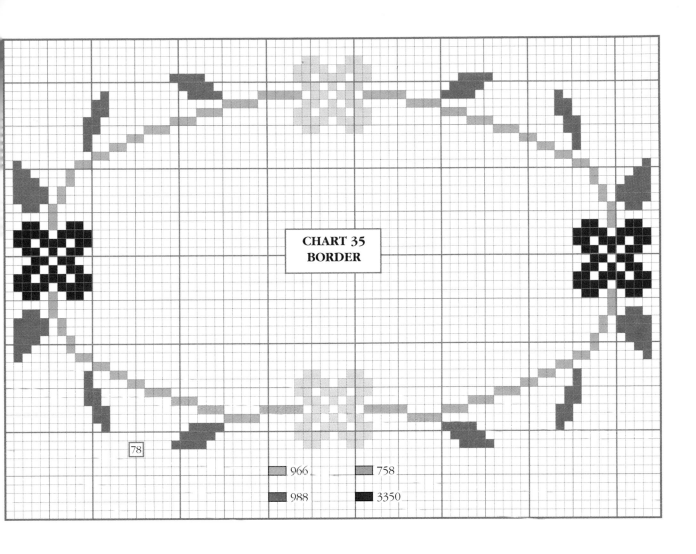

**CHART 35
BORDER**

78

	966		758
	988		3350

BORDERS AND EMBELLISHMENTS

These decorative borders and embellishments make a useful addition to a project, for example on a sampler when embellishing initials or dates. Motifs 74 and 75 were used on the tree sampler on page 41. The plain heart shape (no. 77) was combined with the rose (chart 33, no. 72) to complete the pincushion on page 73. The border on chart 35 was used for the lovely "new home" card – Winterfold Farm – illustrated on pages 104–5.

CHART 35		CHART 36	
*DMC	ANCHOR	*DMC	ANCHOR
327	0872	966	0214
502	0876	988	0262
727	0295	758	0337
501	0878	3350	0896
3350	0896		
945	0311		
937	0263		
350	0334		
352	09		

Four Seasons in a Garden

The archway designs depicting the four seasons – spring, summer, fall, and winter – are illustrated opposite. The following charts provide the basic archway design, and you can add the seasonal detail from the chart as you prefer. The archway designs and A Garden Framed with Roses, illustrated on page 86, are all stitched partly in Designer Silks and partly in DMC stranded floss and therefore involve a slightly different stitching technique.

When you use space-dyed silk thread, each cross should be worked individually rather than in two directions. If you are unable to obtain Designer Silks, any sort of space-dyed thread would produce a similar effect using the technique above. Otherwise, stranded floss could be adapted as follows: group different shades of one color (say, greens or pinks) and pick them at random within the suggested color choice on the chart – thus, pick from the pinks for the flowers and allow the design to grow spontaneously.

CHARTS 36 and 37

*DMC	ANCHOR	*DMC	ANCHOR
975	0355	738	0372
304	047	561	0218
898	0381	937	0263
640	0393	433	0357

SEASONAL BELLPULL

The bellpull here is stitched on a linen band, but it could just as well be stitched on any even-weave fabric. If a band is used, the stitch count must be checked carefully; as you will see from the illustration opposite, the garlands fit the band perfectly!

CHARTS 38 and 39

*DMC	ANCHOR	*DMC	ANCHOR
834	0874	936	0846
727	0295	712	0387
743	0298	3350	0896
722	323	335	041
554	097	898	0381
327	0872	433	0357
BLACK	0403	304	047
605	074	WHITE	01
3364	0260	977	0313
772	0259		

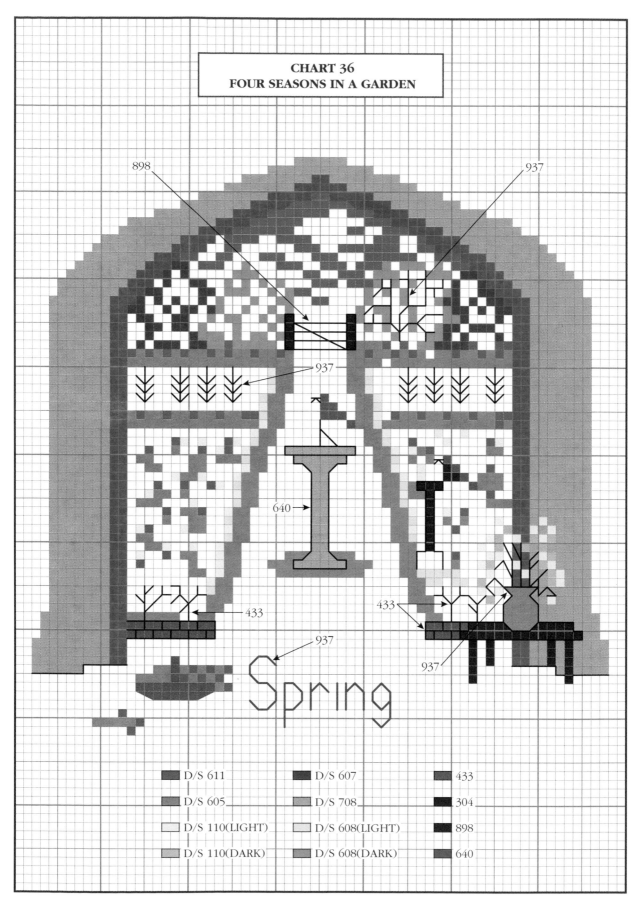

CHART 36
FOUR SEASONS IN A GARDEN

898

937

937

640

433

433

937

937

Spring

D/S 611	D/S 607	433
D/S 605	D/S 708	304
D/S 110(LIGHT)	D/S 608(LIGHT)	898
D/S 110(DARK)	D/S 608(DARK)	640

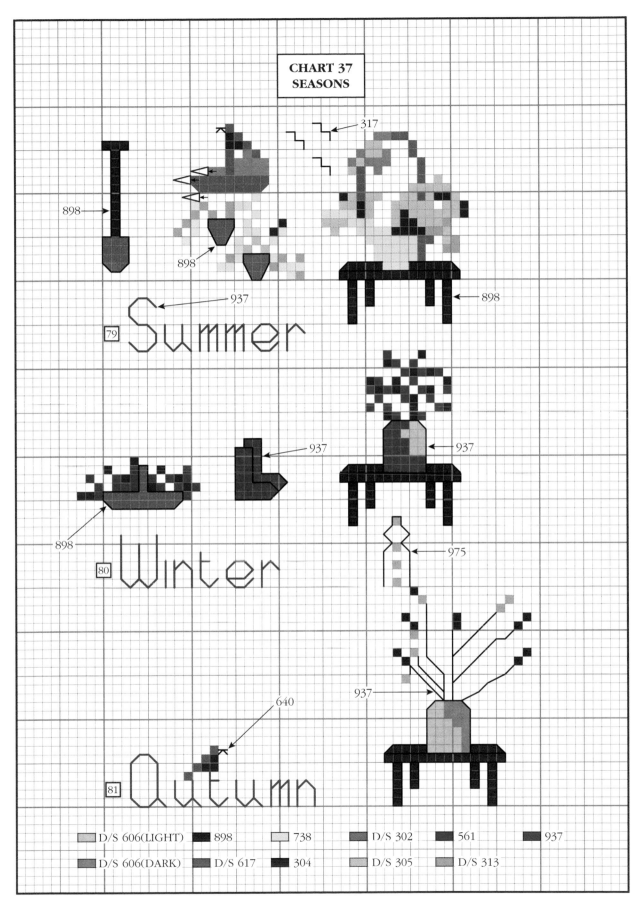

**CHART 37
SEASONS**

317

898

898

937

79 Summer

898

937

937

898

937

80 Winter

898

975

937

640

81 Autumn

| | D/S 606(LIGHT) | | 898 | | 738 | | D/S 302 | | 561 | | 937 |
| | D/S 606(DARK) | | D/S 617 | | 304 | | D/S 305 | | D/S 313 | | |

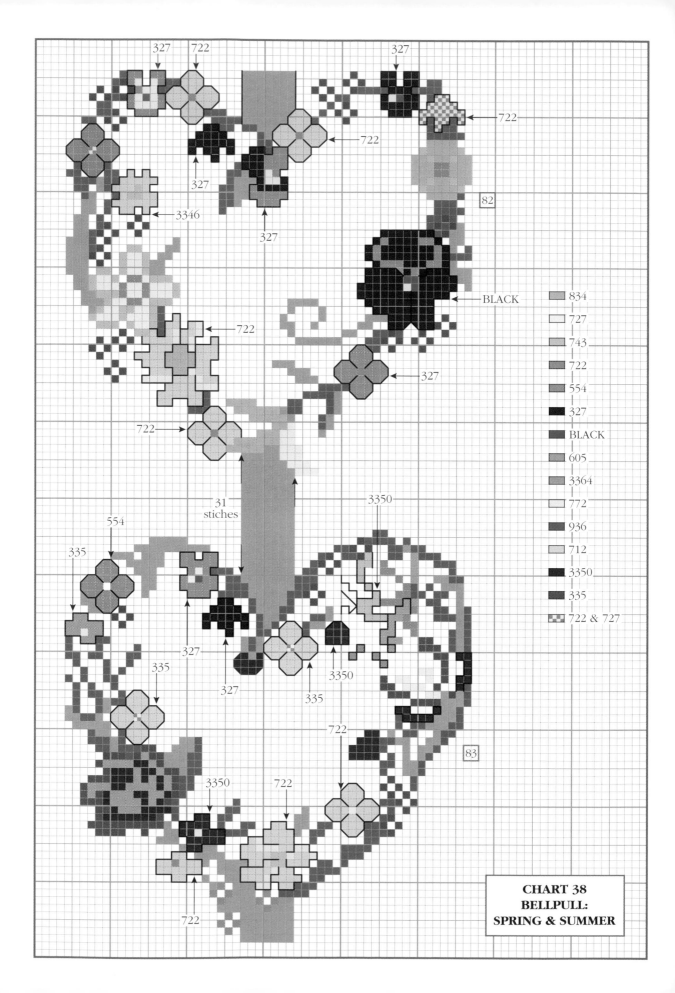

327 722 327

722

327

3346

327

82

722

BLACK

327

722

31
stiches

3350

554

335

327

335

327

722

3350

335

722

335

3350 722

722

834
727
743
722
554
327
BLACK
605
3364
772
936
712
3350
335
722 & 727

83

CHART 38
BELLPULL:
SPRING & SUMMER

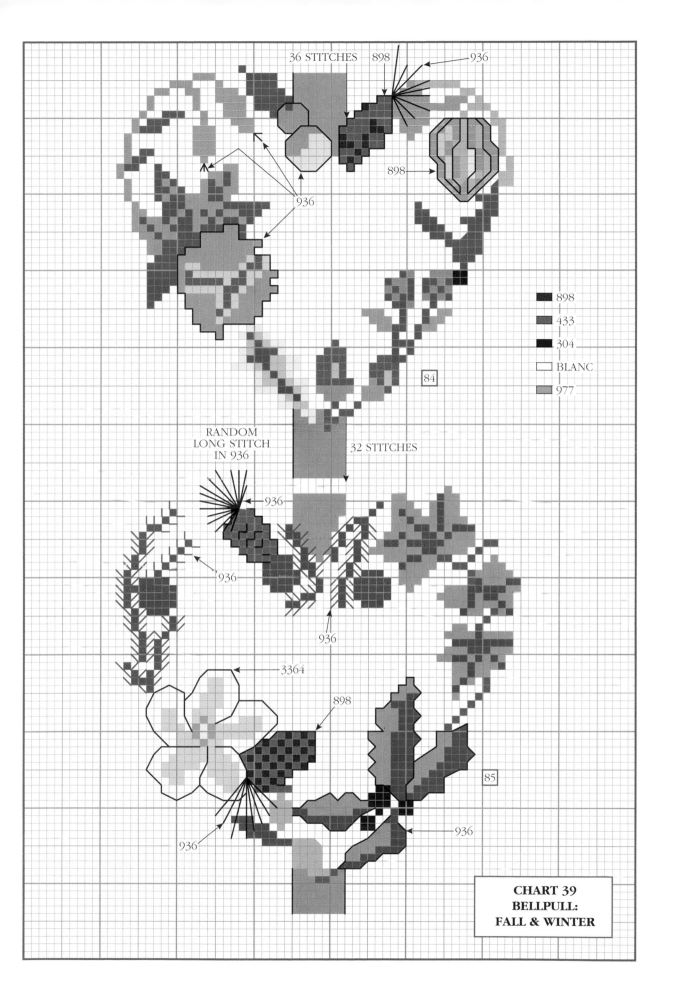

36 STITCHES

898

936

936

898

898

898 | 898
433 | 433
304 | 304
BLANC | BLANC
977 | 977

84

RANDOM
LONG STITCH
IN 936

32 STITCHES

936

936

936

3364

898

85

936

936

**CHART 39
BELLPULL:
FALL & WINTER**

A Garden Framed
with Roses

As already mentioned, this design is stitched partly in Designer Silk. To obtain the shaded effect from the silk, work each cross stitch individually rather than in two directions. To stitch the picture as illustrated, work the house first, stitching toward the pillars at the outer edge. Turn to the rose arch chart (opposite) and work upward. Do the same on the other side, joining the arch at the top by stitching the leaves and roses at random.

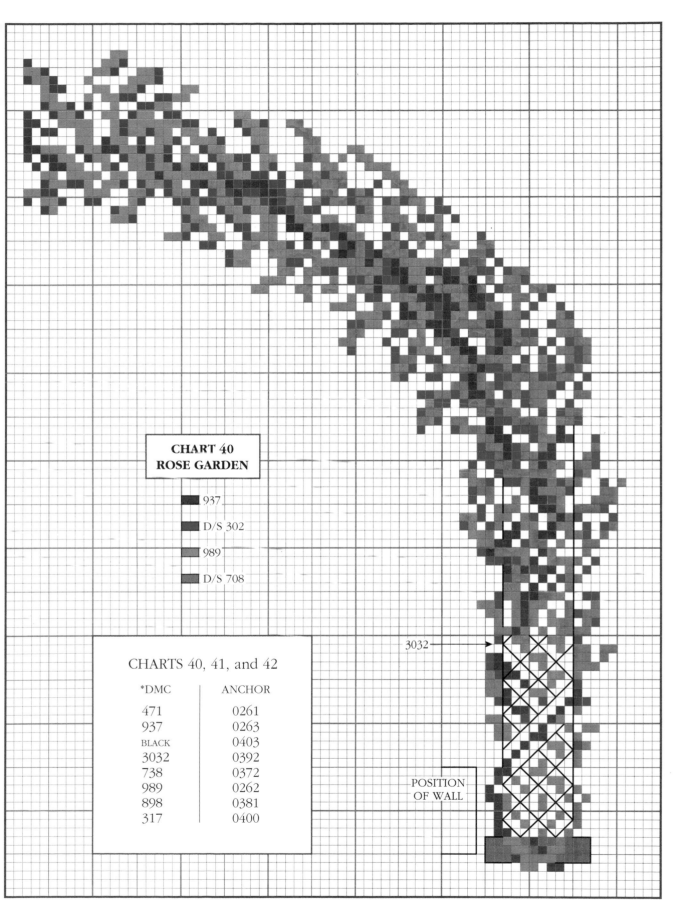

**CHART 40
ROSE GARDEN**

937

D/S 302

989

D/S 708

3032 →

POSITION
OF WALL

CHARTS 40, 41, and 42

*DMC	ANCHOR
471	0261
937	0263
BLACK	0403
3032	0392
738	0372
989	0262
898	0381
317	0400

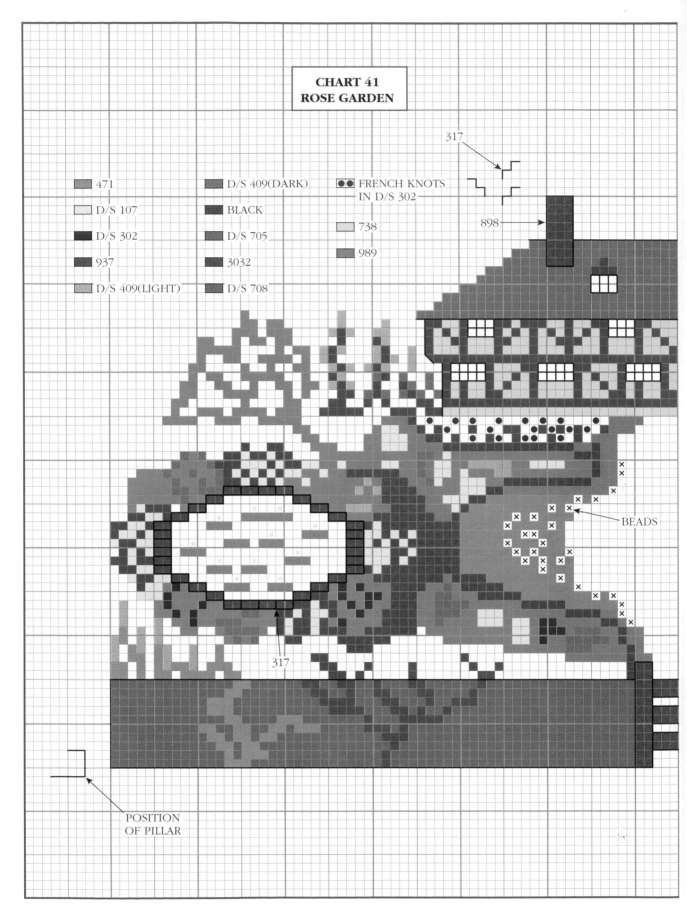

CHART 41
ROSE GARDEN

471

D/S 107

D/S 302

937

D/S 409(LIGHT)

D/S 409(DARK)

BLACK

D/S 705

3032

D/S 708

FRENCH KNOTS
IN D/S 302

738

989

317

898

BEADS

317

POSITION
OF PILLAR

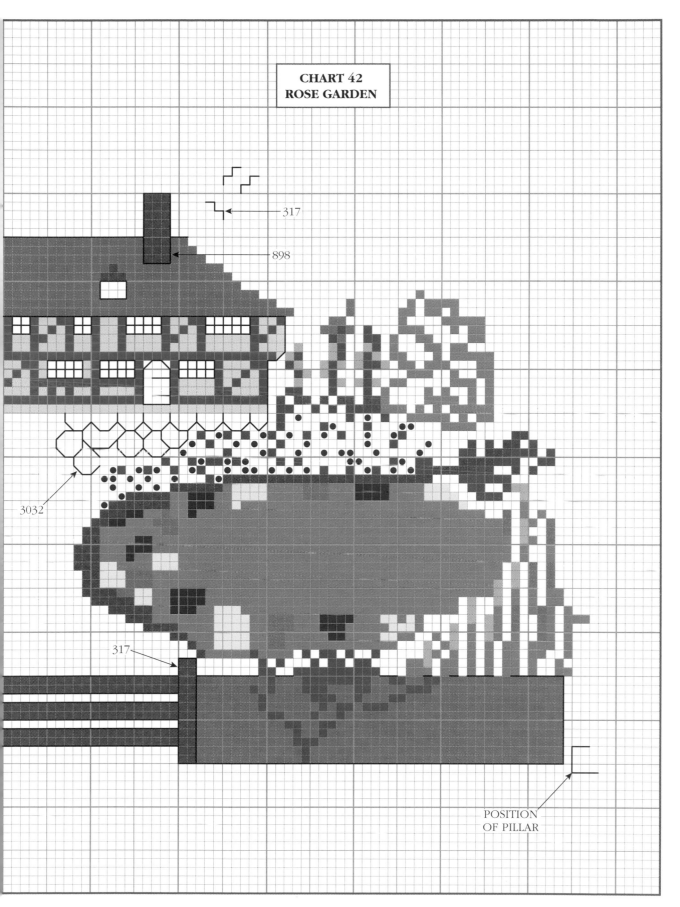

**CHART 42
ROSE GARDEN**

317

898

3032

317

POSITION
OF PILLAR

Country Cottages

"THE OAKS"

This design is one of a number of pretty cottages illustrated in the lovely picture on pages 94–95. This traditional black-and-white beamed building is a good example of its type, and appropriately named, given the surrounding oak trees and its oak beams both inside and out! "The Oaks" is illustrated twice, once in the wooden frame and again as part of the English cottage bellpull.

In both cases, the cross stitch was stitched in stranded floss, using two strands for the cross stitch and one strand for the backstitch outline where appropriate.

CHART 43

*DMC	ANCHOR
898	0381
BLACK	0403
722	323
436	0373
743	0298
WHITE	01
3032	0392
936	0846
3347	0843
640	0393
920	0339

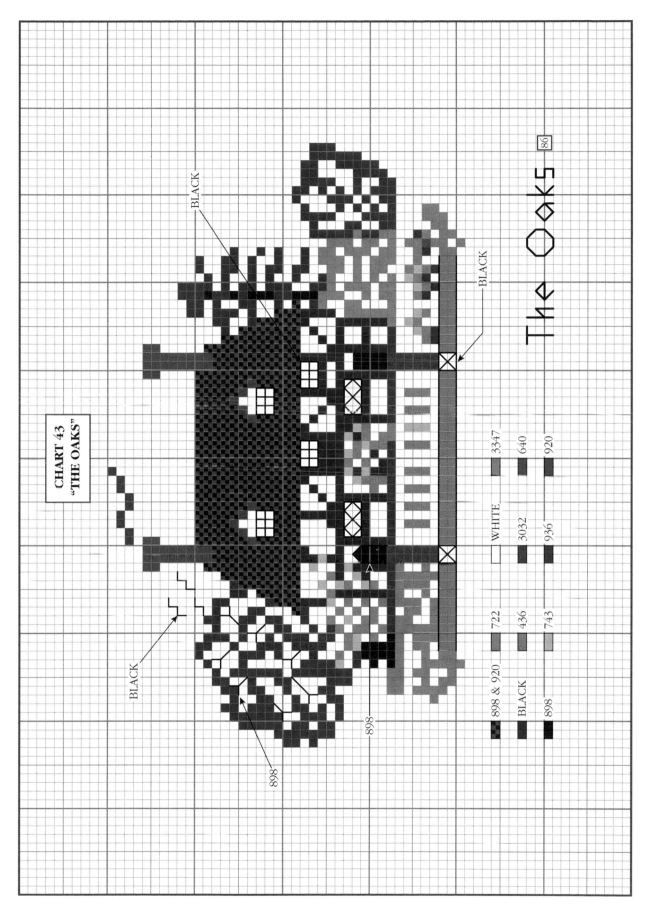

CHART 43
"THE OAKS"

BLACK

BLACK

BLACK

898

898

The Oaks

86

	898 & 920		WHITE		3347
	BLACK		3032		640
	898		936		920

	722
	436
	743

"WILLOWS"

This pretty thatched cottage was based on the mill at Alresford in Hampshire, England; seen in the morning light, it is evocative of an Old Master painting.

CHART 44

*DMC	ANCHOR
562	0216
966	0214
758	0337
792	0123
727	0301
898	0381
739	0361
738	0372
3032	0392
433	0357

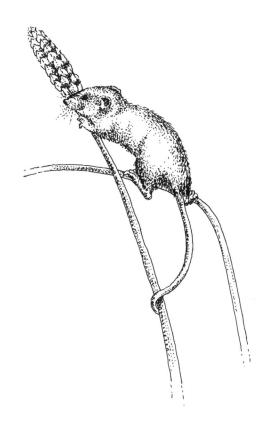

PAGES 94–95
The English cottage bellpull. Clockwise from top left:
"Moor Farm Cottage," "Rose Cottage," "The Oaks,"
"Willows," "Old Barn House," and "Crabapple Farm"

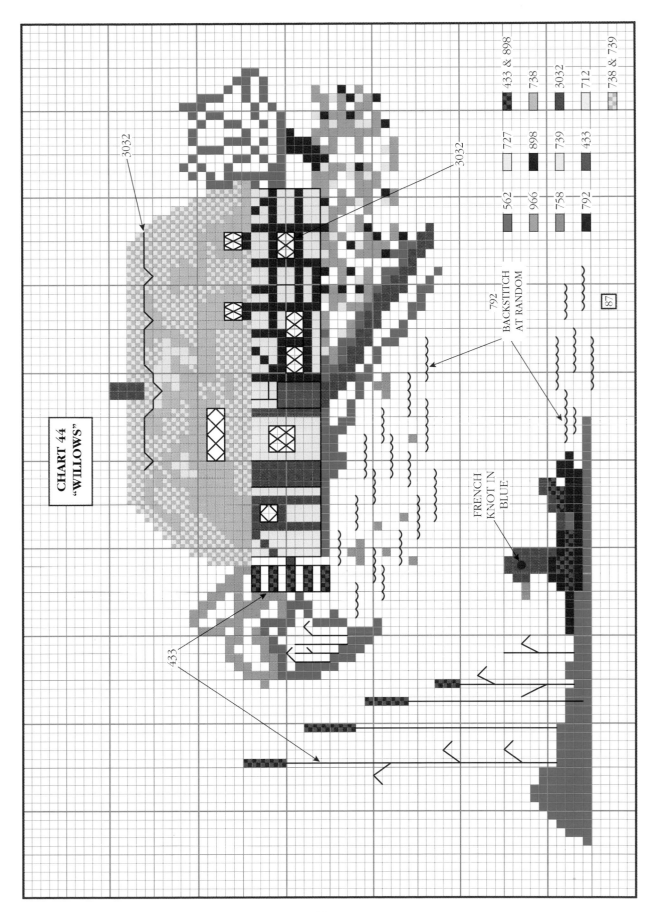

CHART 44 "WILLOWS"

3032

3032

792
BACKSTITCH
AT RANDOM

87

FRENCH
KNOT IN
BLUE

433

562	727	433 & 898
966	898	738
758	739	3032
792	433	712
		738 & 739

English Cottages

Rose Cottage

Moor Farm
Cottage

Old Barn House

The Oaks

Apple
Cottage

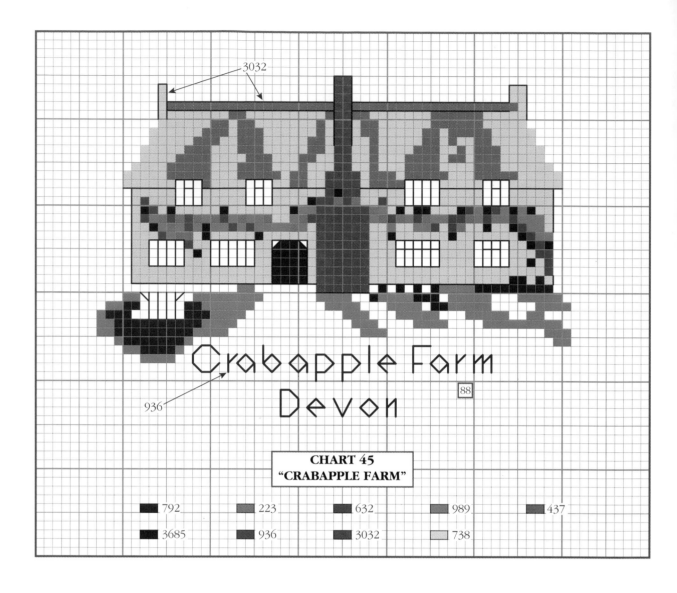

"CRABAPPLE FARM"

"Crabapple Farm" is seen stitched and assembled on page 94; note that a covered mat is used. The idea of making your own mats for pictures is an attractive one; it is both cheap and effective, and adds an original touch to your projects. Basic instructions for the technique are given on page 116 (also see Fig. 8).

CHART 45

*DMC	ANCHOR	PATERNA
792	0123	542
3685	0897	901
223	0895	904
936	0846	600
632	0379	472
3032	0392	463
989	0261	604
738	0372	444
437	0362	445

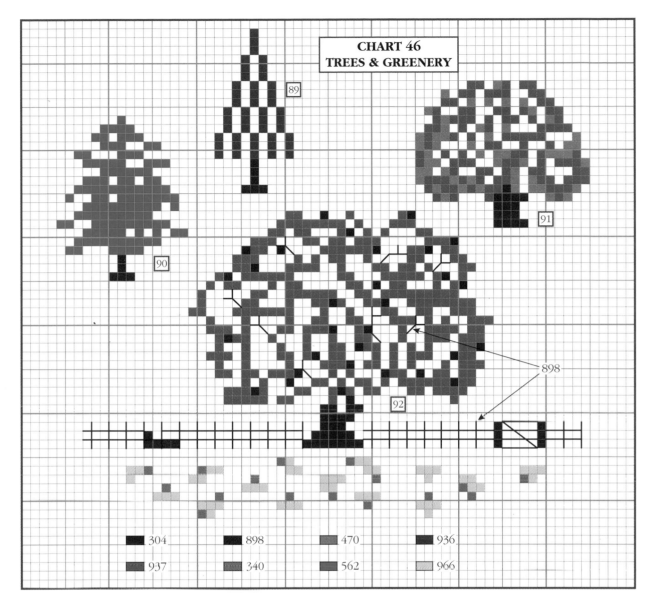

TREES AND GREENERY

The cross stitch on this chart has been worked in two strands of floss, with the fence and outline on the tree worked in backstitch using one strand only. Tree motif 92 can be seen in the picture on pages 50–51.

CHART 46

*DMC	ANCHOR	PATERNA
304	047	950
937	0263	610
898	0381	430
340	0118	343
470	0281	693
562	0216	662
936	0846	600
966	0214	614

"OLD BARN HOUSE" AND "APPLE COTTAGE"

The following charts show the design for four of the charming cottages stitched on the English cottage bellpull illustrated on page 95. They are all sewn on a linen band in stranded floss, using two strands for the cross stitch and one for the backstitch outline.

"Old Barn House" was based on a barn conversion in Gloucestershire, and "Apple Cottage" was inspired by the apple orchards of Kent.

CHART 47

*DMC	ANCHOR	GFT	PATERNA
937	0263	3902	601
3348	0254	2000	612
3350	0896	2088	902
3354	074	1002	905
301	0349		722
738	0372	2003	444
414	0399	1400	201
712	0387	1000	262
642	0392	1500	463
938	0382	1712	421
436	0373	3302	443
437	0362		405
318	0400	1450	212

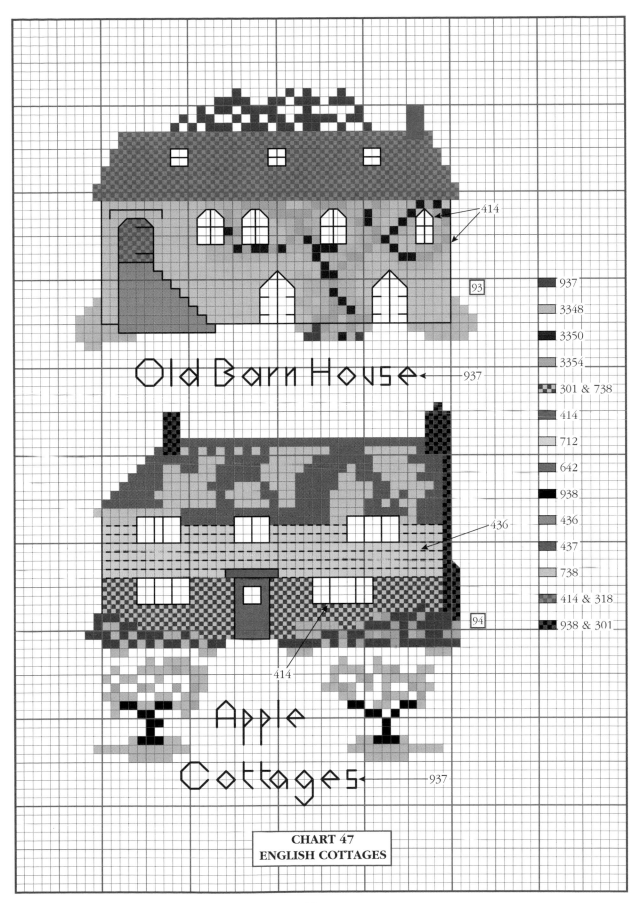

Old Barn House

414

937

93

937

3348

3350

3354

301 & 738

414

712

642

938

436

437

738

414 & 318

938 & 301

436

414

94

Apple

Cottages

937

CHART 47
ENGLISH COTTAGES

"MOOR FARM COTTAGE" AND "ROSE COTTAGE"

"Moor Farm Cottage" is based on a shepherd's home high on the Yorkshire moors, and "Rose Cottage" nestles among the cornfields of Essex. Moor Farm is illustrated twice, once on the bellpull and once in a flower-printed mat. The instructions for making the covered mats are included in the techniques on page 116 (see also Fig. 8).

CHART 48

*DMC	ANCHOR	GFT	PATERNA
317	0400	1450	200
415	0398	2053	203
932	0850	1022	514
224	0894	1002	905
930	0851	2081	512
936	0846	3902	600
436	0373	3302	442
738	0372	2003	444
3347	0843	2000	613
3350	0896	2041	901
223	0895	3305	904

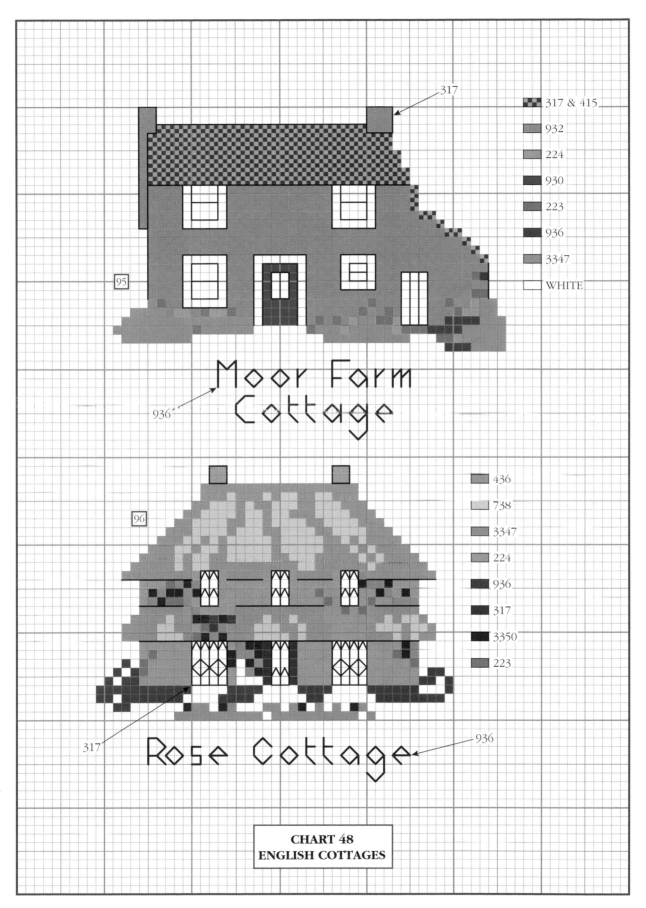

317

317 & 415
932
224
930
223
936
3347
WHITE

95

Moor Farm
Cottage

936

96

436
738
3347
224
936
317
3350
223

317

Rose Cottage

936

**CHART 48
ENGLISH COTTAGES**

Potpourri Sachets

The delightful scented sachets pictured on the overleaf are worked on linen bands, each with a border in a soft contrasting color. The bands are made in Germany from pure linen, and the colored edging is woven into the fabric. The matching tassels are made from the same material as the edging, the perfect complement to each project.

The designs illustrated are stitched in German flower thread, and each sachet is filled with an appropriately scented potpourri. If linen bands are unavailable, strips of any suitable even-weave material could be used.

CHART 49

*GFT	ANCHOR	DMC
1009	0216	562
2099	0259	368
2041	0896	3350
2073	041	335
2088	042	600
1002	075	894
2084	0298	743
3522	0300	727
3832	0210	367
2000	0261	989
2035	0303	742
1049	0304	741
3432	098	553
2011	0112	552
2068	028	961
3215	0850	931
3022	0403	BLACK
2079	039	309
2061	0301	744

PAGES 104–5:
Potpourri sachets and Winterfold Farm card

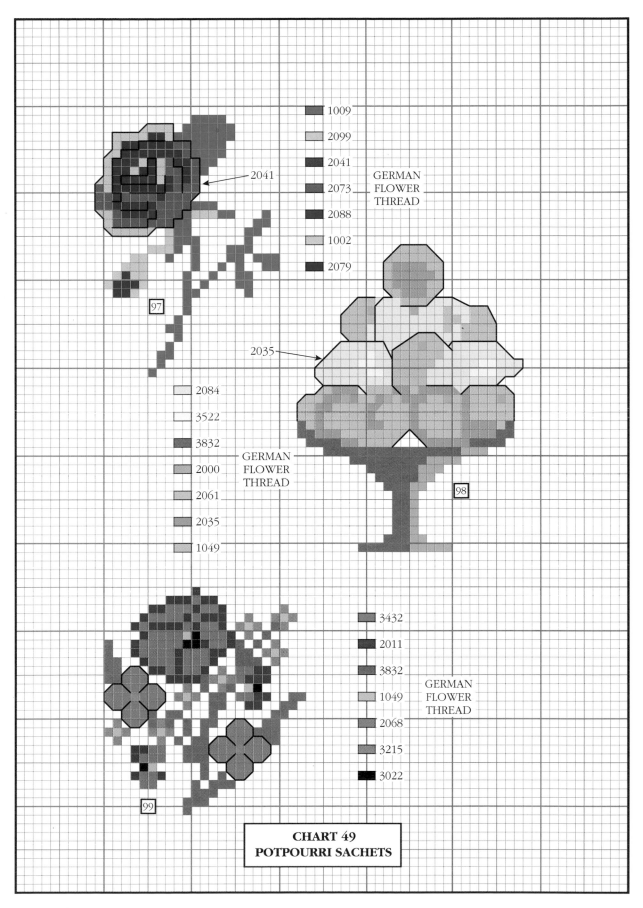

1009
2099
2041
2073
2088
1002
2079

GERMAN
FLOWER
THREAD

2041

97

2035

98

2084
3522
3832
2000
2061
2035
1049

GERMAN
FLOWER
THREAD

3432
2011
3832
1049
2068
3215
3022

GERMAN
FLOWER
THREAD

99

**CHART 49
POTPOURRI SACHETS**

POTPOURRI SACHETS

CHART 50

*GFT	ANCHOR	DMC
3006	01	WHITE
1105	046	349
2088	042	309
2084	0298	743
2082	0300	744
2000	0261	989
3001	0216	562
1005	0112	552
3332	097	554
1007	0393	640
1222	0392	3032
3902	0263	937
1003	0895	223
2023	0400	317
3832	0210	367

FINISHING

When the cross stitch is complete, check for missed stitches and press the needlework on the wrong side. Place the *wrong* sides together, aligning the edges of the linen band, and pin in position. Slipstitch the two edges together with the matching thread. Turn under a narrow hem at the top of both sections and hem invisibly (see Fig. 5).

When the bag is complete, fill with appropriately scented petals and tie with matching flower thread, attaching a tassel at the same time.

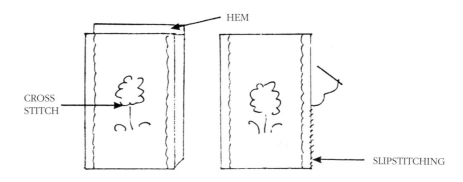

Fig. 5 Making scented sachets

106

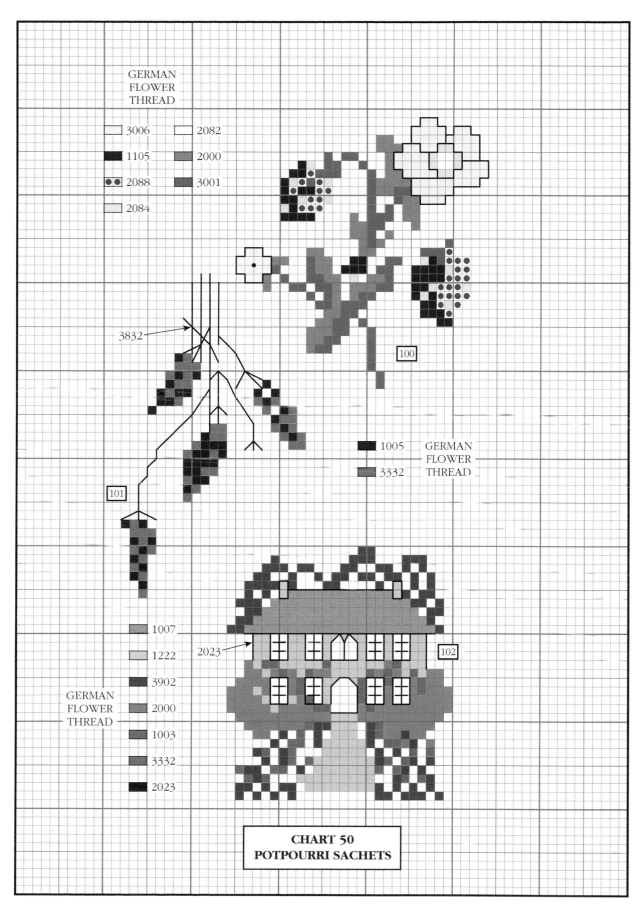

GERMAN
FLOWER
THREAD

3006   2082
1105   2000
2088   3001
2084

3832

100

101

1005   GERMAN
FLOWER
3332   THREAD

1007
1222
2023
3902
GERMAN
FLOWER   2000
THREAD   1003
3332
2023

102

**CHART 50
POTPOURRI SACHETS**

La France

The design for the lovely alpine house pictured opposite uses a selection of spring colors. It could be stitched equally well in the vibrant colors of summer, possibly using some of the excellent rayon threads available.

Charming thatched houses like "Normandie" (also pictured) are dotted all over the Normandy hills, with manicured gardens and the most wonderful irises growing in the top of the thatch. Most of the design in chart 52 is planned for you, but the flowerbeds in the foreground should be worked at random in either cross stitch or French knots – use the color key as a guide.

CHART 51

*DMC	ANCHOR	PATERNA
772	0259	695
320	0261	693
937	0263	691
640	0393	461
611	0832	462
341	0117	505
3033	0388	465
632	0379	472
317	0400	210
743	0298	772
415	0398	212
3032	0392	463

CHART 52

*DMC	ANCHOR	PATERNA
350	0334	843
550	0102	311
210	097	313
758	0337	874
937	0263	601
794	0117	562
435	0369	403
640	0393	462
738	0372	444
744	0301	714
3348	0261	604
223	0895	932

RIGHT:
Les Alpes and Normandie

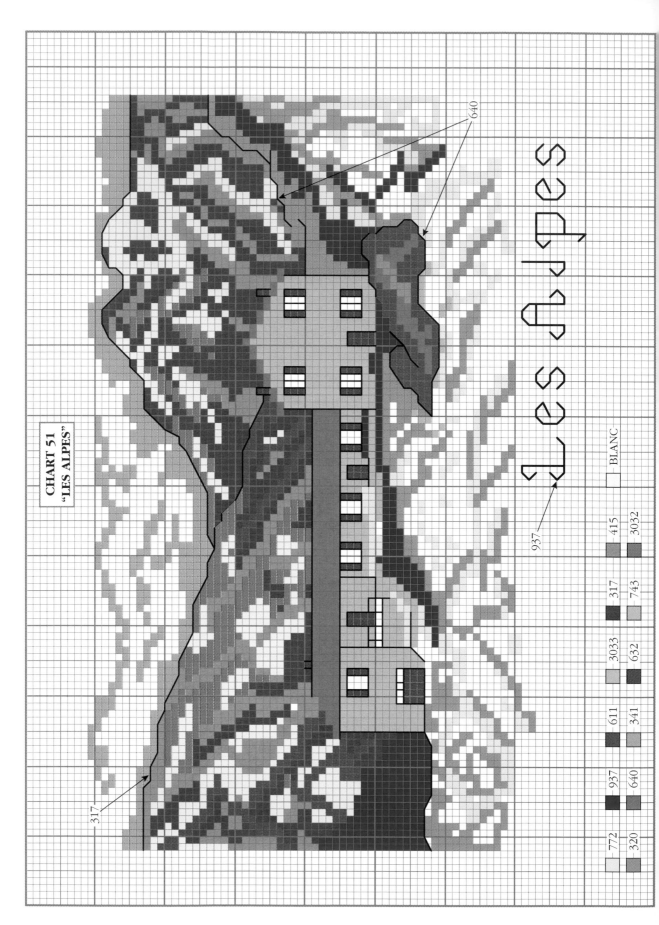

CHART 51
"LES ALPES"

Les Alpes

640

937

317

772	937	611	3033	317	415	BLANC
320	640	341	632	743	3032	

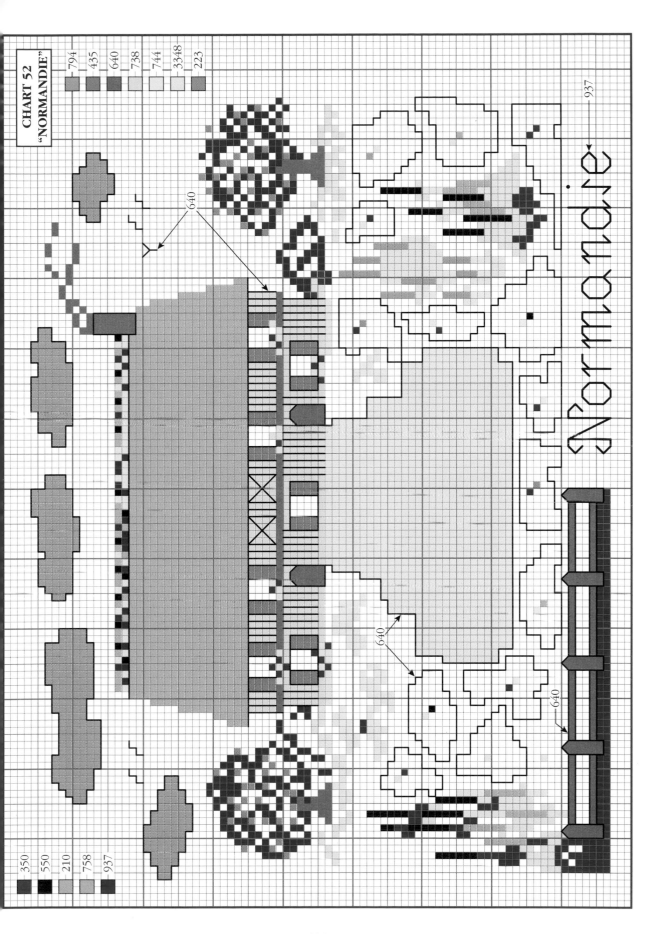

Motifs and Ribbons

ASSORTED MOTIFS

CHART 53

*DMC	ANCHOR	*DMC	ANCHOR
320	0261	501	0878
433	0357	436	0373
349	046	932	0850
304	047	471	0262
223	0895	945	0311
3350	0986	727	0295
898	0381	722	0323

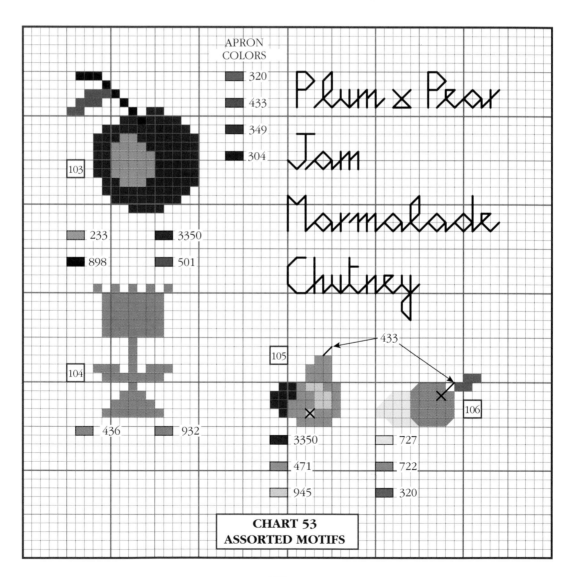

CHART 53
ASSORTED MOTIFS

RIBBONS
CHART 54

*DMC	ANCHOR
772	0259
936	0846
3364	0261
352	09
350	0334
930	0851
932	0850

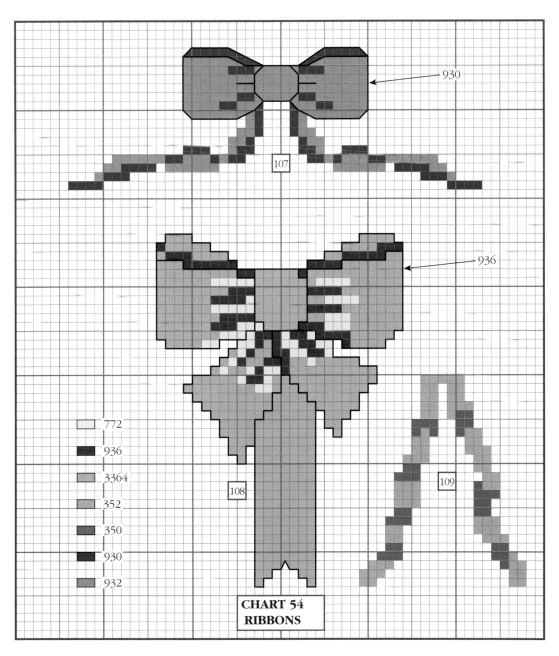

930

936

107

108

109

	772
	936
	3364
	352
	350
	930
	932

CHART 54
RIBBONS

List of Fabrics

The motifs illustrated in this book are stitched and finished in a number of ways, using a variety of fabrics. The list of materials below indicates which fabric was used for each project seen in the color pictures. Feel free to use any even-weave material for your own designs, but always check the stitch and thread count before starting the project.

LINEN: 25 threads to 1 inch (2.5 cm)
Butterfly alphabet
Tree sampler
Bread bag
Wine bag

LINEN: 28 threads to 1 inch (2.5 cm)
Brush and comb set
Black vest
Basket-of-fruit recipe holders and
   picture
Jelly jar labels
Country sampler
"Moor Farm Cottage," "Crabapple
   Farm," and "Rose Cottage"
Black pepper and coffee bean bags
Sea salt (unbleached linen) bag
Christmas rose pillow
Rosebud pillow
Heart rose pincushion
"The Oaks"
"Willows"
Basket-of-fruit clock

LINEN: 30 threads to 1 inch (2.5 cm)
Little alphabet
English village sampler
Four Seasons in a Garden
A Garden Framed with Roses
Christmas rose, and bread napkins

AIDA: 14 blocks to 1 inch (2.5 cm)
Basket noteboard in country Aida
Tree picture
Message board
French hutch card

AIDA: 18 blocks to 1 inch (2.5 cm)
"Les Alpes"
"Normandie"
Butterfly crystal jar

MURANO: 30 threads to 1 inch (2.5 cm)
Country diary
Recipe folder
Louise name plate

LINEN BANDS (see suppliers):
Potpourri sachets in colored bands
Cottage and seasonal bellpulls

MISCELLANEOUS:
Silk thread file in Belfast linen: 32
   threads to 1 inch (2.5 cm)
Footstool in unbleached Belfast linen:
   32 threads to 1 inch (2.5 cm)
Flower throw in Afghan fabric
Apple apron in Sanger products (see
   suppliers on page 119)
Wooden trinket box in 18-count
   single canvas

Useful Techniques

Detailed instructions for cross stitch are not included in this book, but the techniques needed to make the projects pictured in the lovely photographs are given below. All the projects are charted and can be mixed and matched to make new designs of your own, the essential requirement being to observe the stitch count and the thread count of the material.

CARDS

There are many different sorts of blank cards available from craft stores, and these are simple to make into lovely gifts. The finishing techniques for cards will vary, but the following method will suit most brands.

When the stitching is complete, press the design on the wrong side and set aside. Open the folded card completely and check that the design fits in the opening. Apply a thin coat of craft glue to the edge of the opening on the wrong side (see Fig. 6). Add the design, carefully checking the position of the stitching, and press down firmly. Fold the spare flap inside and secure in place with either double-sided tape or another thin application of glue. Allow to dry before closing.

Fig. 6 Making a card

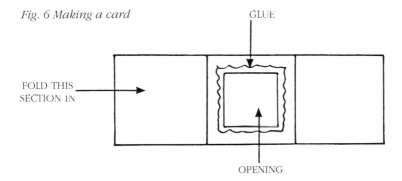

STRETCHING AND MOUNTING

When mounting small cards or novelty projects, the whole procedure can be completed using double-sided tape, but it is worth taking more time and effort on larger projects. You will need either acid-free mounting board or light-weight foam board, or you can cover a piece of board with a natural fabric like cotton which can be anchored with rubber cement and left to dry.

There are three methods of attaching the needlework to the board before framing (see Fig. 7):

1 Pin the work to the edge of the board and secure in place with double-sided tape;
2 Pin to a covered board and stitch in position;
3 Pin to the board and lace across the back with strong linen thread.

Whichever method is used, when you pin the material to the board first make sure it is centered and stretched *evenly* because any puckers will show when the design is framed. Measure the board across the bottom edge and mark the center with a pin. Match this point to the center of the bottom edge of the embroidery and, working out from the center, pin through the fabric, following a line of threads, until all four sides are complete. Then attach it (Fig. 7), either by stitching through the needlework to the covered board, or lacing the excess material across the back, or anchoring with double-sided tape.

COVERED MATS

The simplest piece of needlework is given dimension by adding a covered mat to coordinate with the design (see Fig. 8, page 117). If you intend to use an oval or circular-shaped mat, you will certainly need to buy it, as it is almost impossible to cut these yourself. Square or rectangular mats can be cut using a utility knife, as the rough edges will be covered by the material.

Press the embroidery on the wrong side, and stretch and mount as described above. Cut the mat board the same size as the mounted embroidery and cut an opening of the size you require. If the mat has been purchased, check that the opening is large enough for the embroidery and set aside.

Referring to Fig. 8 for the following method, use the mat as a template, and cut a piece of patterned material at least 1 inch (2.5 cm) wider all the way around. Place the material right side down on a clean flat surface and, using a soft pencil, draw around the inside of the opening. Remove the mat and, using a sharp pair of pointed scissors, cut out the opening about ½ inch (1.25 cm) from the pencil line; clip the edge at intervals. On the wrong side of the mat, apply a thin layer of glue to the edge of the opening and add the material, checking to make sure the pattern is straight. Glue down and allow to dry. Complete the procedure by pinning and securing the excess material as for stretching and mounting the embroidery on the backing (Fig. 7).

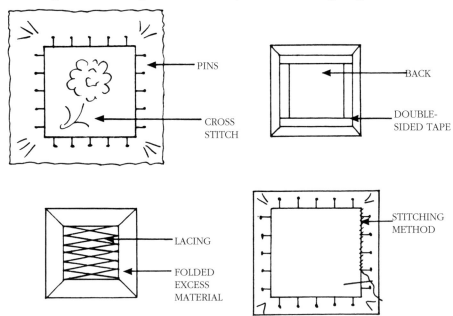

Fig. 7 Stretching and framing

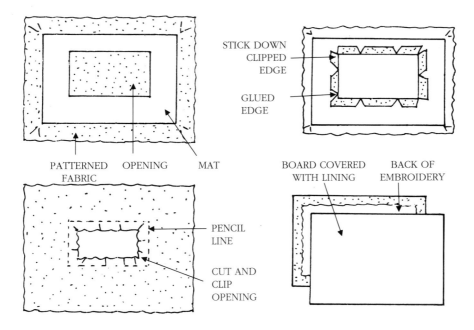

Fig. 8 Making covered mats

MAKING FOLDERS

If you intend to make the completed project into a folder, you will need to line the inside as well. Cover a piece of this board with the same or coordinating material as described above and when dry, slipstitch to the inside (see Fig. 8). Ribbons may be added at this point to make hinges or fastenings (see picture on page 65).

To make folders, there are two methods which can be used: the scoring method, when the folder is made up in one piece (Fig. 9), and the stitching method, when the folder is made in individual sections which are then joined together (see Fig. 10). In both cases, a softer look can be achieved by covering the board with batting before assembling (see Fig. 9).

When the stitching is complete, press on the wrong side and set aside.

The Scoring Method

Refer to Fig. 9 (page 118) for this method. You will need a piece of heavy cardboard (mat board is ideal) large enough to make the front, back, and spine of the folder. Lay the board on a clean flat surface and, using a sharp utility knife, score as illustrated, then fold the board, thus forming the spine.

Open the board again, lay it on a flat surface, and cover it with a slightly larger piece of batting; lay it on the board with the embroidery, checking the position of the stitching – you must also make sure the original piece of fabric is large enough to wrap around the board in one section. Pin, using the method described in stretching and mounting, then trim the excess material away, leaving 1 inch (2.5 cm) around the edge; secure this with strips of double-sided tape. Pressing gently on the scored areas as you work, fold the front and back up to check that the fabric is secure, then set aside while the lining is prepared.

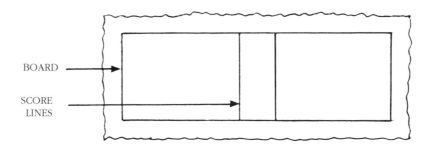

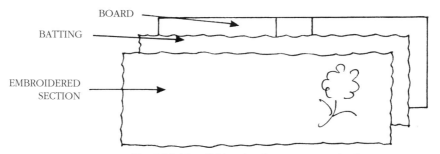

Fig. 9 Making folders by the scoring method

Cut a piece of coordinating material for the lining at least 1 inch (2.5 cm) larger than the completed book, fold the raw edges inside, and slipstitch in position.

Stitching Method

Referring to Fig. 10, you will need three pieces of board: the front, back, and spine. To cover them, you will need the embroidery, a matching piece of fabric for the back, and a strip for the spine. Cut a piece of lining material and batting to match each section. The idea is that you make a three-layer sandwich with the lining, board, batting, and the embroidery or back section. To make one section, proceed as follows: Lay the lining right side down on a flat surface, and lay the board on top. Add the batting and then the embroidery right side up. Fold the raw edges under, and slipstitch invisibly all the way around.

Compete all three sections in the same way, and finally stitch all three pieces together using matching threads.

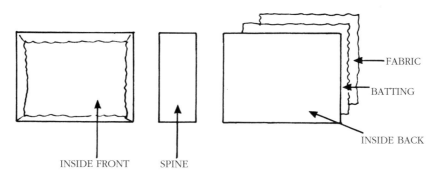

Fig. 10 Making books in three sections

Acknowledgments

I would like to thank the following people and organizations for all their help and support allowing me to write this, my third cross stitch book: first, my husband, Bill, whose financial management and sales expertise has helped The Inglestone Collection to thrive during a recession!

A very special thank you to Michel Standley, without whom the production at The Inglestone Collection would grind to a halt and who still has time to run her home, bring up a family, stitch, and keep me organized!

To the Inglestone team, who keep the business running all the year round – Jean, Daphne, Thelma, Rita, Emma, Liz, and Diane; also all the staff and trainees at Newholme Day Centre and the Adult Opportunity Centre at Cirencester.

To my dedicated stitchers, without whose addiction this book would not have been possible: Dorothy Presley, Angie Davidson, Hanne Castelo, Di Fallows, Elizabeth Lydan, Vera Greenoff, Caro Lebez, Tamsin O'Brien, and Pat Beadle.

To my dear frined Ursula Joka-Deubelius for her hospitality, inspiration, and her beautiful German flower thread. Also Rosalind Parnell, whose continued interest in my exploits is as surprising as her fluent German has been invaluable. And all the staff at Vaupel and Heilenbeck, Germany, for their hospitality and their patience with my complete lack of German.

A special thank you to Sara Jane Gillespie, Yew Tree House, Symonds Yat West, for sparing the time in her busy schedule to draw the delightful pen and ink sketches that fill this book; to Di Lewis for reading my mind when doing all the lovely photographs; and to Vivienne Wells, who continued to have faith in me when others would have given up.

I would also like to thank the following companies for the advice and supplies used in this book: Cara Ackerman from DMC Creative World for generous supplies of fabric and threads; Tunley and Son for framing and art supplies; Framecraft Miniatures Ltd. for trinket boxes, brush and comb sets, trays, and frames; and MacGregor Designs, Burton-on-Trent for wooden pincushions, footstools, and trinket boxes. Also Sanger Linen, Switzerland for the red apron; and Wheatland for the acetate clock.

The beautiful pillows on pages 68–69 were made by Sue Hawkins' excellent finishing service at Needleworks in Cheltenham, England.

Thanks also to the following for needlework supplies: Campden Needle-craft Centre, Chipping Campden, Glos; The Ladies Work Society, Moreton-in-Marsh; Knatty Designs, Stow-on-the-Wold; Tikkit, Gloucester Docks; and Cirencester Needlecrafts. Also Artisan Pinner for printed fabrics and needle-craft supplies.

Index

Page numbers in *italic* refer to illustrations

English Cottages

Rose Cottage

Moor Farm Cottage

Old Barn House

The Oaks

Apple Cottage